# Mediated Access
# Broadcasting and Democratic
# Participation

# Mediated Access:
# Broadcasting and Democratic Participation

Brian McNair, Matthew Hibberd,
Philip Schlesinger

UNIVERSITY
OF LUTON

press

British Library Cataloguing in Publication Data

A catalogue record for this book is available from the British Library

ISBN: 1 86020 592 5

Published by
University of Luton Press
University of Luton
75 Castle Street
Luton
Bedfordshire LU1 3AJ
United Kingdom

Tel: +44 (0)1582 743297; Fax: +44 (0)1582 743298
e-mail: ulp@luton.ac.uk
website: www.ulp.org.uk

Cover Design Gary Gravatt, Gravatt Design Consultancy
Typeset in Van Dijck MT
Printed in United Kingdom by Thanet Press, Margate UK

# Contents

# Preface and Acknowledgements

At the beginning of the twenty-first century the relationship between the media and democracy is high on the political and public agenda. Perceptions of a crisis in democratic participation, and of significant failings in the political media which exist to support democracy have produced a flurry of debate on the current state of British political journalism. The BBC's *Beyond the Sound Bite* (Kevill, 2002) and Hargreaves and Thomas' *New News, Old News?* (2002) study for the Independent Television Commission and the Broadcasting Standards Commission are among recent attempts to identify the deficiencies of political broadcasting in the UK, and to suggest ways in which they might be rectified. Such work is part of an ongoing effort which seeks to identify, as Entman and Bennett put it in their edited volume on *Mediated Politics* (2001), "the communication conditions that either promote or discourage broad citizen engagement".

The research reported in this book aims to contribute to that effort, by focusing on one particular type of political communication – the forms of public participation broadcasting we group together in our title as *mediated access*. Our aim in the following chapters is to assess the contribution political access programmes make to British democracy, as seen from the perspectives of their producers, their audiences sitting at home, and those members of the public who make up their participants, whether as members of a studio audience, callers down a phone line, or e-mailers on the internet.

Our conclusions are encouraging, in so far as our research shows that the provision of mediated access to politicians and political debate is regarded by producers, politicians and audiences as a potentially valuable tool in the re-engagement of public interest in and enthusiasm for democratic processes. We also, however, identify the need to support those broadcasters who wish to protect and strengthen the spaces for political access programming which currently exist in British broadcast schedules, and to do so within a framework which recognises the difference between the legitimate ambition of political journalism to be popular, and the commercially-driven demand to be populist. At a time of intense competitive pressure on all broadcasting organisations, we wish to add our voice to the argument that, at a time of perceived public cynicism about and apathy for institutional politics, well-designed political broadcasting of quality – access programing in particular – can indeed play a role in strengthening democratic participation.

Running through the study is a key question: what makes a good access programme, given the normative role participation is expected to play in the public sphere, and the political, economic and technological conditions within which it is produced? While there will always be a strongly subjective dimension to the many different answers which might be given to that question, we aim in this book to contrast the measurable aspirations and achievements of radio and television producers with the perceptions of the public – both participants and audiences - about what has been achieved.

The authors are members of the Stirling Media Research Institute, based in the department of Film & Media Studies at Stirling University. The research presented here builds on previous work in the fields of political communication and of public participation broadcasting carried out by the authors (McNair, 2000; Schlesinger et al, 2001; Hibberd et al, 2000), and was funded by the Economic and Social Research Council as part of its Democracy and Participation programme (project reference L215252016). Our thanks go to the programme director Professor Paul Whiteley for his support and encouragement throughout. While predominantly a political science programme, the inclusion of this media studies project in the Democracy and Participation initiative reflects the fact that the contemporary study of politics is, to say the least, incomplete without careful and adequately-resourced research into the political media and how they relate to the democratic process. We hope that this example of such research, and the findings we present below, will be of value to both the political and media studies communities, as well as professional broadcasters, politicians and all those members of the public who share an interest in the present and future health of mediated democracy in the United Kingdom.

We express our sincere gratitude to all those broadcasters, politicians and members of the public who participated in the research by granting interviews or participating in focus groups. Special thanks go to the producers of *Channel 4 News* at ITN, with whom we collaborated in a study of users of broadcaster web sites. That investigation was not part of the work for which we were funded by the ESRC, but emerged as an opportunity in the course of our interviews with broadcasters. We report the findings of that study in chapter six. We would also like to acknowledge the contribution of those broadcasters, journalists and academics who participated in the symposium organised by the authors at Stirling University in January 2002. Their comments on our work, and their contributions to the debate that day, are reflected in this volume.

BRIAN MCNAIR, MATTHEW HIBBERD, PHILIP SCHLESINGER
STIRLING, FEBRUARY 2003

# 1

# Broadcasting and Democratic Participation in the Age of Mediated Politics

For some time now observers of British politics have identified a 'crisis' of democratic participation, measured by such indices as falling rates of party membership, reduced involvement in political campaigning and, most urgently, a decline in voting. Only 24 per cent of the eligible electorate participated in the United Kingdom's 1998 European parliamentary elections, with turnouts falling below 20 per cent in many parts of the country. Voting in local elections, never very high in the UK, has fallen to historically low levels in recent times. The turnout of 59 per cent recorded at the 2001 general election – the lowest since 1913 – seemed to confirm the downward trend in democratic participation, and produced renewed warnings of a broader crisis of political legitimation on the horizon. If people don't vote, it is argued, it may be because they have no confidence in their democratic institutions. When so many citizens lose confidence political parties find their mandate undermined, and the entire system of governance begins to lose credibility.

These phenomena are not restricted to the UK, but are a feature of many mature democracies throughout the world. The 2000 presidential election in the United States was not the first in that country to have recorded a less than 50 per cent turnout. The outcome in that case was further complicated by the fact – albeit a quirk of the US voting system rather than a consequence of low turnout in itself – that the winning candidate, George W. Bush, secured fewer votes than his Democratic challenger, in a contest accompanied by allegations of vote-rigging and procedural irregularities in the state governed by the Republican candidate's brother, Jeb Bush. Had the terrorist attacks of September 11th 2001 not intervened to put the USA on a war footing, it seems likely that the country would have faced four years of more than usually weak executive leadership following the indecisive 2000 vote. Britain is still some way from general elections in which less than half of the population exercise their right to vote (although in 2001, to the alarm of many, more constituencies than ever before recorded lower than 50 per cent turnouts), but few dispute that the British trend, like that of the US, has been downward for some time.

In mainland Europe, too, recent elections have produced lower than expected turnouts, and some uncomfortable outcomes for established political elites. In the French presidential elections of 2002 a low turnout allowed the National Front candidate, Jean-Marie Le Pen, to force the incumbent, Jacques Chirac, to a second-round ballot, while the Socialist candidate, Lionel Jospin, was humiliated. In Holland, the libertarian populist party of the late Pym Fortuyn achieved dramatic successes against established parties which had failed to mobilise their traditional supporters at the polling booths. If the defeat of Austria's far-right Freedom Party in November 2002 (and indeed the eventual defeat of Jean-Marie Le Pen in France) suggests that these trends are far from universal, and certainly not irreversible, they remain a feature of political life in many advanced capitalist societies.

While the recent decline in rates of formal political participation is an empirical fact, its causes and meanings are far from clear. Some observers take a relaxed view of what they interpret as benign civic apathy; evidence not of 'crisis' but of broad public satisfaction with the state of things. In Britain, it is argued from this perspective, as some have suggested was true of the United States in the 1990s, a buoyant economy has produced a mood of general contentment amongst the electorate. 'If it ain't broke' under New Labour – and, falling stock market prices notwithstanding, with unemployment, inflation and interest rates all at record low rates in early 2003, there was little substantial evidence that anything really *was* broke – why try to fix it by tampering with the make up of the board of directors?

It is generally accepted that Labour's victory in 1997, and its political dominance since, has been reinforced by the weakness of the Conservative Party which, as this book went to press, seemed unlikely to be a serious contender for government in the short term. Voter apathy, it is suggested in this analysis, is encouraged by a government which is doing well, and by the lack of a credible alternative for those who might be inclined to opt for one. A related argument is that in the de-ideologised, declassed atmosphere of Tony Blair's new millenial Britain, policy differences between the major parties have become so marginal that more people than ever before genuinely feel it doesn't matter which one they vote for.[1]

Some have explained declining turnouts by suggesting that the British people are overdosing on democracy. With European elections every four years, a devolved parliament and assemblies now up and running in Scotland, Wales and Northern Ireland, English regional assemblies on the horizon and elected mayoralties in London and other cities it is argued that there are just too many elections for all but a dedicated minority of the British people to follow with anything like the enthusiasm of the less-enfranchised past, when voting was still something of a novelty, and thus an event worth making an effort for. Increased opportunities for democratic participation have exposed the awkward fact that many people consider themselves to have better things to do with their free time than queue up at polling stations.

Disputing that the average citizen's appetite for democracy is as modest as the above explanations would imply, more critical observers see declining participation as an index of deep dissatisfaction with politics; one manifestation of a conscious withdrawal from the democratic process by unprecedented numbers of people. Research undertaken by the Hansard Society in the aftermath of the 2001 General election showed that 60 per cent of young people did not vote. The research also concluded that for many non-voters, 'not voting was something they had chosen to do: a positive abstention rather than apathy' (Diplock, 2001).

From the intellectual left this dissatisfaction is usually blamed on the inegalitarian, socially exclusive nature of capitalism itself, and the existence of large numbers of people who feel themselves to have little or no stake in the system. Not voting is seen from this perspective as a rational act of dissent or protest, a gesture of defiance against a system in which the voter has no real stake. Jean Baudrillard's *In the Shadow of the Silent Majorities* (1983, p.10), now more than twenty years old but still resonant in an era when democracy expands but democratic participation declines, welcomes the fact that 'the masses resist this imperative of rational communication'.

Others, both left and right, blame the crisis of democratic participation on what is argued to be the increasingly shallow, banal content of political discourse; a banality made more off-putting by the intensity with which it is packaged and promoted through the machinery of political public relations now employed by all parties. Voter apathy, from this perspective, is a direct consequence of the relentless spin which surrounds policy pronouncements; of the sound-bites and photo-opportunities which today comprise so much of public political rhetoric; of the use of political marketing and focus groups in the formulation and presentation of policy.

And in this communicative dimension of the crisis, the media – as the main disseminators and translators of political discourse to the citizenry – are held to be complicit. The current downward trend in democratic participation is often attributed to failures and inadequacies in the performance of the political media; what Jay Blumler and Michael Gurevitch have characterised, in their book of that name, as the 'crisis of public communication' (1995). By this is meant a journalistic departure from the normative ideals of the fourth estate as defined by political philosophers from Edmund Burke to Jürgen Habermas. Many critics, both journalistic and academic, have identified a 'dumbing down' of mediated political culture, reflected in an increased fascination with the 'trivia and fluff' of political affairs (such as the personal images and private lives of politicians) as opposed to the serious and the substantial (Franklin, 1994, 1997). Peter Dahlgren has recently articulated this view, writing that 'by any standards of evaluation [the public sphere] is in a dismal state' (2001, p.35). 'The ideals of journalism', he continues, 'are increasingly subordinated to the imperatives of the market' (Ibid., p.36).'The public service mission of journalism', writes another critic, is being undermined by the "intertwining of news with marketing goals" (Underwood, 2001, p.100).

Commercial pressures, it is argued, have fuelled an excessive journalistic focus on insider issues, and an over-reliance on opinion pollsters and spin doctors as sources of political news and analysis. Political journalism has become shallow and incestuous, as ill-informed speculation by a new breed of special correspondents replaces hard reporting, and as star interviewers like John Humphrys and Jeremy Paxman become steadily more hyper-adversarial and arrogant. In all of these ways and more, the political media are alleged to promote public apathy and cynicism, turning people off not just politics, but the coverage of politics. Reinforcing this analysis, for some, is the fact that broadcast news coverage of the 2001 general election hit record lows in ratings terms,[2] prompting the BBC to embark on a critical review of their output with the aim of re-engaging viewers, especially the young, in political subject matter (Kevill, 2002).[3]

These protestations of crisis in public communication can themselves be criticised as manifestations of the cultural pessimism which has long been a prominent feature of scholarly analysis of the political media. As we and others have argued (McNair, 2000; McNair, Hibberd, Schlesinger, 2002; Hargreaves and Thomas, 2002), less doom-laden interpretations of the trends in political journalism are possible. The rise of the adversarial political interview, for example, may be read as the victory of infotainment or presenter-vanity, and also as a logical and welcome journalistic response to the growth of political public relations and spin. Indeed, the two readings are not incompatible. The well-briefed, carefully-rehearsed political interviewee needs a tough, even rude and quite possibly vain interviewer if he or she is to be compelled to divulge anything other than propaganda and rhetoric to the audience.

Likewise, the oft-criticised growth of process journalism as against coverage of policy – coverage of style over substance – need not be denounced as dumbing down, but may be interpreted as a potentially valuable deconstruction of the political process in an era of intensely professional political communication management. If the modern politician is more likely than ever before to be a skilled media performer, packaging his or her messages in pretty, if disposable wrap, political journalism has become to some extent a review medium, although not at the expense of what some call 'hard' political news. Hargreaves and Thomas' report on broadcast news for the ITC/BSC (2002) showed that what they categorised as domestic politics, international affairs and social/economic stories comprised between 55 and 80 per cent of news output on British TV in 2001, depending on the programme (*Channel 4 News*, for example, with its more analytical, in-depth style, had more political coverage than, say, early evening ITV bulletins).

Our aim in this book, however, is not to rehearse once again that seemingly endless debate[4] about trends in the political public sphere as a whole. And even if space allowed, such a discussion is not necessary to the arguments which follow, because even amongst some of its most fervent critics there is acknowledged to be a ray of hope in the evolution of the political public sphere; a counter to the negative trends which are often argued to characterise the media-driven crisis of public communication. This positive counter-trend is the growth of *public participation* broadcasting, or *mediated access* to political debate, by which we mean those forms of TV and radio programming – complemented by internet channels, text messaging on mobile phones, and interactive digital technologies – through which citizens are enabled to be physically present in the public sphere, encouraged to state their views on political issues, to debate them with professional experts of various kinds, and to question representatives of the political elite face-to-face in ways which, the programme makers hope, amount to significant participation in the democratic process.

Public participation programming has become a major element of television and radio output in many democratic countries. In Britain and the US, where the genre was pioneered, the biggest audiences go to day-time talk shows like those hosted by Oprah Winfrey and Robert Kilroy-Silk, which involve audiences in discussion of a wide range of human interest and lifestyle subjects. Some of these debates may have relevance to party politics, when for example they raise questions of social policy or law and order which it is the remit of governments to address. Others are less about immediate political choices than they are discussions of subjects like sexual and identity politics. But either way, and assuming that topics like domestic violence, racism and homophobia are of real public importance, such programmes are clearly fora for political discussion and argument. A lively debate has developed around the cultural role of these programmes, with proponents defending their ability to provide a presence in the public sphere for previously excluded or marginalised groups (Shattuck, 1997; Gamson, 1998). Critics, on the other hand, have pointed to the rise of the broadcast 'freak show' (Dovey, 2000; Ast and Mustazza, 1997) as evidence of the commercially-driven degeneration of the public sphere.

Again, we do not in this book address the fascinating and important issues raised by the popularity of day-time talk shows. With the exception of *The Wright Stuff* (a hybrid programme combining discussion of topical political issues with a broader human interest agenda, broadcast by Channel 5) we have not included such shows in our study, focusing instead on access programmes which focus on the issues of government and civic administration debated in the public sphere by parties and serving politicians, elected representatives, single-issue groups and lobbyists. Fencing off these debates from the discussion of, for example, domestic violence or sexual abuse which might take place on Oprah or Kilroy is by no means to suggest that the latter are of lesser relevance to, or importance in the public life of a society. Indeed, we have previously written at length about talk shows, docu-soaps and other forms of public participation programming – what has been called 'reality TV' – and have drawn on that work in the design of the research for this book.[5] But in so far as the crisis of democratic participation is generally seen as a problem of party politics, and the processes of governance, this study is centred on programmes which explicitly address formal, institutionalised politics.

While for obvious reasons only a small number of individuals can take part in these programmes directly, as studio participants or phone-in callers, many millions more watch and listen to them at home. They, through their watching and listening, are invited by the programme makers to think of themselves as participants in political debate, and as citizens with a stake in the political process. Some variants of the form make this explicit by encouraging audience participation and feedback through post-programme telephone calls and electronic voting, the results of which may be fed back into the content of subsequent programmes, or become the subject of political journalism and debate elsewhere in the public sphere.

There are more of those programmes on UK television and radio than ever before; more, too, than are found in any comparable democracy, covering a variety of formats from the recorded studio debate to the live phone-in show. The research conducted for this book set out to explore how, and with what degree of success as judged by the various actors involved – producers, participants, and members of the public – the democratic aspirations of mediated political participation are being realised. It considers the extent to which the various forms of mediated access spread across the TV and radio schedules can play a role in mobilising individuals to take a greater interest in public affairs. Does the fact that access programmes are often broadcast live, for example, and if not live then 'as live' (recorded and transmitted in relatively unedited form) mean that they may be thought of as part of what Chambers and Costain (eds., 2000) call 'deliberative democracy'? Deliberative democracy – which we take to mean active, participatory democracy that involves debate and disucssion – requires inter-active, two-way channels of communication between the citizenry and the political elite. It also presumes that members of the public are in a position to use those channels intelligently. Can British access programming be said to display those characteristics, and thus contribute to what Chambers and Costain characterise as 'a healthy public sphere where citizens can exchange ideas, acquire knowledge and information, confront public problems, exercise public accountability, discuss policy options, challenge the powerful without fear of reprisals, and defend principles' (ibid., p.xi)?

For many observers the answer to this question is a resounding yes. Sonia Livingstone and Peter Lunt have welcomed the emergence of what they call 'talk show democracy' (1994) in the UK, while Kenneth Newton speculates on the positive role of public access programmes in the 'mobilisation' of the citizenry, and their contribution to the construction of an informed, participatory public sphere (1997). In the United States an expanding body of research is examining patterns of participation in TV and talk radio shows which address overtly political topics, including those which do so under the direction of idiosyncratic and extreme 'shock jocks' (Herbst, 1995; Barker, 1998; Jones, 1998). Even as they criticise the provocative, reactionary manner in which some of these programmes handle the issues under discussion, analysts note that they comprise the only media spaces in the USA where ordinary members of the public can have their say on the issues of the day, political and otherwise, and that this gives them potential value as democratic instruments; makes of them, indeed, 'talk show democracy'.

'Forum media', as Douglas Rushkoff calls access broadcasting, 'however sensationalised or tabloid it may get, depends upon the interpretive and evaluative skills of its audiences, even if it does not demand knowledge of facts or history' (1996, p.65). While dissociating himself from the on-air rantings of the shock jocks, Rushkoff defends access shows generally on the grounds that they are 'participatory'. In contrast to the tradition of top-down journalistic spoon-feeding of news to passive audiences eating their TV dinners at home (as Rushkoff characterises the producer-consumer relationship associated with the majority of news and current affairs media) access programmes, on TV and radio, 'call upon the intelligence of [their] viewers and participants' (ibid.). Moreover, they 'loosen the grip of public relations experts on the opinions of the greater population'. Rushkoff here turns the familiar criticism that contemporary political discourse is excessively managed on its head, contrasting the spun-ness of traditional news media with the relatively raw and unspun character of access programming. In the era of the sound-bite and the photo-op, he suggests, and to the extent that it breaks through the professionally crafted rhetoric to the political reality underneath, public participation programming acquires an enhanced value. Jonathan Freedland's *Bring Home the Revolution* (1998) also celebrates the democratising power of US talk shows. Indeed, he contrasts them favourably with the more controlled, rule-governed tradition of access in the UK. From an Australian perspective, dominated in this area of political broadcasting by US-style radio talk shows, as well as a limited tradition of televised studio debate, Catharine Lumby argues:

> The traditional media formats and journalistic values are not value-free – they're grounded in a top-down model of public debate in which experts and others 'in the know' decide which issues are important and proceed to explain and debate them on behalf of 'ordinary' people. In contrast, the tabloid end of the media spectrum, from radio talkback to daytime talk shows ... is characterised by the opinions and stories of people with no claim to expert knowledge. Chaotic, populist, and populated by demagogues though this end of the media sphere may be, it's also the place you can most often hear ordinary people speak out on their own behalf (1999, p.xii).

Only some of the British access programmes examined in this study could be described as 'tabloid' in the sense intended by Lumby and Rushkoff, since they straddle all the main TV and radio news channels, from BBC Radio 4 and Channel 4 to ITV and Radio Five Live. They have at times been chaotic, however, even populist (see the 1997 Monarchy debate, discussed below), in contrast to the studied impartiality of the British public service broadcasting tradition, and have been criticised as such. Some implicate access programming in a broader 'videomalaise' caused by the political media in general, and express deep pessimism about the capacity of public participation programming in particular to contribute usefully to the democratic process. Pierre Bourdieu denounced French political access broadcasting as a 'charade' (2000), fuelled by commercial rather than democratic motives. For Bourdieu, the need to entertain means that political journalists seek 'confrontations over debate' and 'prefer polemics over rigorous arguments' (ibid., p.5). Debates staged before public audiences become spectacles comprising 'populist spontaneism and demagogic capitulation to popular tastes' (ibid., p.48).

For another brand of critic, the fact that all access programmes are, by definition, arenas for *mediated* politics conducted at various removes from what they would characterise as 'reality', undermines their participatory value. Robert Putnam's influential study of the decline of civic culture in America, *Bowling Alone*, argues that 'TV-based politics [and, by extension, radio and internet-based politics] is to political action as watching *ER* is to saving someone in distress. Just as one cannot restart a heart with one's remote control, one cannot jump-start citizenship without face-to-face participation. Citizenship is not a spectator sport' (2000, p.41).

Indeed it is not, and in making mediated access to political debate the subject of this work we do not wish to suggest that an individual's engagement with political broadcasting as a member of a media audience can, or should be, an acceptable substitute for participation in voting, campaigning, membership of a party or other forms of political activity outside the domestic environment of the home. On the contrary, we wish to better understand the extent to which it can be viewed as *another form* of democratic participation, additional and complementary to 'real' politics, which the rise of mass communication in the latter part of the twentieth century has made possible for the first time. We do, however, contest from the outset Putnam's apparent assumption that the process of media spectatorship is less than real, and does not require a degree of cognitive engagement with the activities being watched (or listened to); that cognitive engagement with the competing political positions expressed in a broadcast debate is not in itself a kind of democratic participation, of real political significance in an age of mass mediation.[6] It is self-evident, we would suggest, that information received from the media, in whatever form, can become part of the cognitive environment within which an individual reaches conclusions and makes political choices.

We also challenge the related assumption – central to the pessimism of Putnam and like-minded observers – that mediated access to politics (access mediated through TV, radio or any other channel of electronic communication) is in some way necessarily inferior to the interpersonal, face-to-face mode experienced by past generations of voters (who were, of course, a minority of the population as a whole), when politicians would tour the country and participate in hustings meetings at which they might be robustly challenged and heckled. These encounters, valuable though they no doubt were to those who had access to them, were limited of necessity to audiences of a few hundreds or thousands at most. The great majority of the people had no involvement in them beyond the journalistic accounts they read in their newspapers (those who could read, that is) or hear on the conversational grapevine.

The tradition of political speech-making at public rallies has declined, of course, and where such encounters still take place they are more often than not controlled with tight precision by public relations and communications professionals whose job it is to prevent unscripted moments of reality intrusion, such as the occasion during the 2001 general election when deputy prime minister John Prescott punched an egg-throwing protester. Such exceptions aside, public speaking engagements tend nowadays to be part of a broader media campaign in which the appearance of public access to the politician concerned may be deceptive. Mediated political debate, by contrast, typically reaches millions of people watching or listening to TV and radio in their own homes, providing access to their politicians which is often live and unedited. In undertaking this study we reject the presumption that those millions are less likely to be informed, motivated or mobilised into action by what what they see and hear on public participation broadcasting than would have been the nineteenth-century crowd at a hustings meeting, struggling to hear the content of a political speech delivered without the aid of electronic amplification by a man on a podium hundreds of feet away.

Our starting point as communication scholars is that the modern electronic media, and their penetration into the domestic environments of virtually the entire population, in a context of universal suffrage, allow for the transmission of political messages which have the potential to be just as intimate and affecting as the interpersonal exchanges of the past, and may indeed be more real to the average citizen than the latter ever could have been.

Having stated our belief in the *potential* importance of mediated political debate, we do *not* therefore assume that individuals are more likely to participate in 'real' politics (by voting, for example) if they do so first in mediated contexts, whether as studio participants or as members of the viewing and listening audience. As already noted, the refusal to vote need not be interpreted as non-participation in democracy, so much as another *kind* of participation – the active exercise, for whatever reason, of the right not to vote. Making such a choice could be an outcome of watching or listening to a public participation programme, and learning from it that, for example, 'they're all as bad as each other', or 's/he is defensive and evasive, as opposed to honest and open'. Although we report our findings on the political backgrounds and motivations of those who participate directly in public access broadcasting, whether by joining studio audiences or making calls to phone-in programmes, our research did not set out to establish a positive correlation between mediated political participation and propensity to vote. We do, on the other hand, assess the extent to which those members of the public who participated in the study *feel* that they have had meaningful access to, and opportunity to engage in, political debate through their involvement in these programmes. What they choose to do with the information they have acquired in such contexts, and how those feelings translate into political action, is a question for further research.

## A Note on Method

Our approach in this study has been to start from what the programme makers say they are *trying* to do; to identify their production goals and their aspirations in respect of the democratic process, before considering the extent to which these are realised in practice, and the factors assisting (or constraining) them in their efforts to do so. These factors fall into three broad categories, arising from trends in: (a) the *political culture* within which public participation is organised at any given time; (b) the *economic environment* as it impacts on the production of political media; (c) the *technological infrastructure* available to broadcasters.

### Politics

An important trend in political culture, for example, has been the changing relationship between people and power in post-World War II British society. This has been a product of processes such as the rise of feminism and its impact on the place of women in British society, and the similarly increased status and visibility of ethnic minorities, the gay community, the disabled, and other excluded or marginalised groups. It incorporates the process of constitutional devolution embarked upon by the Labour government after its election in 1997, with all its implications for the development of the UK public sphere (see chapter three). Above all, it reflects the gradual erosion of many of the class, status and taste distinctions which underpinned social deference in the UK for decades after World War II. The effects of declining deference have been observed – not without criticism, as we have noted – in many sub-sectors of the public sphere, such as the increased intrusiveness of journalism on the private affairs of elite groups, and the heightened aggressiveness of the political interview. Chapters three and four consider the impact of these trends, and other aspects of a changing political culture, on how producers construct access programmes for a population which is, in historical perspective, more diverse (socially, sexually, and ethnically), better informed, better enfranchised and less inclined to doff its collective cap to assumed privilege than any before it.

### Economics

The evolution of public participation programming is not just an index of broader political and socio-cultural change, but of change in the economic environment and the structure of the media industries. The first British political access programme of the modern type went on air in 1948 (see Chapter two), at a time when the publicly-owned, licence-fee funded BBC monopolised broadcasting. More than half a century later TV and radio channels have proliferated through terrestrial, cable and satellite lines. The new channels are commercially funded, with obvious implications for their scheduling strategies. And given the proliferation of channels, even the commercially-protected BBC has been obliged to pay more attention to its competitive position than ever before, putting extra pressure on the producers of news and current affairs programming to justify their place in the schedules. In this context, the ethos of consumerism rubs against the more traditional public service ethos of citizenship. Media academic Steven Barnett argues that 'in the history of the BBC there has never been more pressure from commercial competitors to justify virtually every kind of output in which the organisation is involved, nor more commercial desire to see the BBC retreat into a backwater of public service elitism'.[7] As for the commercial channels, head of news for the ITV network, Steve Anderson, observes that 'with the proliferation of competition it is going to get harder and harder to carry on doing the public service side of the business. In order to do it we're going to have to think of new ways of making [political] programmes, getting people's attention, making the programmes relevant.'[8]

Many critics point to the marginalisation of broadcast current affairs journalism on both BBC 1 and ITV, exemplified by the movement of the flagship *Panorama* current affairs magazine to a Sunday night 'graveyard' slot, and the disastrous (for its ratings) shifting of the long-established *News At Ten* indulged in by ITV scheduling managers in 1999/2000. Access programmes continue to claim a place in the schedules, however, at least for the present, buoyed up by evidence such as that presented in Sian Kevill's *Beyond the Soundbite* report for the BBC, which found that people wanted greater accessability in political broadcasting (2002). Hargreaves and Thomas' ITC/BSC-funded study of 4,000 respondents found that 'the type of programme which received most favourable mention was the format which allows the ordinary viewer to interrogate a politician or someone famous. Viewers also speak warmly of television programmes which hold power to account' (2002, p.67). The focus group research carried out for this book reached similar conclusions on what viewers want.

That said, the steadily more competitive economic environment faced by broadcasters means that access programmes must pay their way in ratings terms. We examine below how, and with what success, the broadcasters have attempted to reconcile the need to command large audiences with what they acknowledge to be the democratic aspirations of access programming.

## Technology

The development of mediated access, and the capacity of its producers to fulfil their stated goals, has also been affected by the onward march of new interactive technologies – most recently e-mail, the world wide web, and the mobile phone. Chapter Six relates the efforts of political broadcasters to integrate these new technologies into their programmes. It considers, in particular, the efforts of the producers of *Channel Four News* to develop a programme-related website.

## The Research

Our main methodological tool was the semi-structured in-depth interview. Seven political broadcasting strands involving public participants were selected (see below) and we interviewed programme-makers and participants from each. We also interviewed programme-makers from another eight radio and television programmes, and undertook interviews with broadcasting executives and politicians to ascertain their views on the democratic role of mediated access. The politicians came from the Conservative, Labour and Liberal Democratic parties, and included a former Minister and one current party leader. The broadcasters interviewed included the respective Heads of News and Current Affairs for Channel 4, Channel 5 and ITV.

A number of one-off access programmes were included in the study, such as the ITV's monarchy debate broadcast in 1997, and the same channel's *Ask the Prime Minister*, broadcast in December 2000. Access programmes broadcast by BBC 1 and Channel 4 in late 2002 to facilitate public debate on the then-mounting Iraqi crisis came too late to be studied in-depth for this book, but we have referred to them where appropriate.

Programmes selected for study covered all five main terrestrial television channels and the satellite channel, Sky News. Our radio programmes came from the two BBC network stations, Radio 4 and Radio Five Live and from BBC Radio Scotland. We also interviewed programme-makers from the local commercial channels Scot FM (radio) and Scottish television.

We sought, where possible, to select programmes from different parts of the radio and television schedules, including two morning programmes, one mid-evening, and one late-evening.

Although many of these programmes were produced in London and the Southeast, we were also able to speak to programme-makers in Scotland, the Midlands and East Anglia. A total of thirty programme-makers were interviewed for the project. Of these, twenty were of senior producer level (executive producer or series producer), and ten were production staff responsible for contacting participants (producers, associate or assistant producers and researchers). Four presenters were also interviewed. Although the main part of each interview concentrated on the specific programme under study, interviewees were also encouraged to talk about other programmes on which they worked, or had worked in the past.

## Interviewing participants

An important element of the project was to speak to members of the public who had participated in access programmes about their experiences. Each programme-maker granted us permission to speak with participants (when they were members of the studio audience) or to telephone them (when they were participants in phone-in programmes). As far as possible, we tried to speak to participants of different age groups, from different regions or nations within Britain, and from different socio-economic and ethnic backgrounds. We were also able to interview participants with a wide variety of occupations. A total of forty public participants were interviewed for the project. While the central focus of each interview was on the participant's perceptions of his or her contribution to the programme under study, we also asked them whether they had been involved in other political access programmes and/or political activities.

## Focus groups

Interviews with broadcasters, programme-makers, politicians and participants were complemented by a series of six focus group meetings held in London, the South East and Scotland with members of the general public. These locations were chosen not just for logistical reasons, but because data from our previous study into public participation (Hibberd et al, 2000) revealed that Scotland was among the nations and regions with the highest viewing figures for radio and television programmes, whereas London was among the lowest. We calculated, therefore, that focus groups from these two areas would offer a broad range of opinions and comments.

Participants in the focus groups were selected to provide a broadly representative demographic sample of the public, and a few had experience of participation in access programmes.

The focus group discussions addressed audience attitudes to public participation broadcasting in general, and evaluations of specific programmes, extracts from which were played to the groups. Each focus group was shown four clips from programmes and was then asked a set of questions relating to each programme.[9]

## The Programmes

The programmes selected for this study do not include all public participation programmes currently found in British broadcasting, although they do encompass key examples of this kind of output, including the flagship programmes of the main channels, BBC1 and ITV. They represent UK-wide and local access formats, programmes on radio and television, public service and commercial channels, and the range of formats utilised by British broadcasters at the time when the research was undertaken.

Four radio programmes were selected.

*Any Questions?* is the longest running political access programme on radio. The programme is billed by BBC as Radio Four's 'forum for lively debate between decision-makers from all areas of public life', and is chaired by the broadcaster, writer and environmentalist, Jonathan Dimbleby. It is broadcast live from a different location each Friday evening at 8pm, usually at the behest of local community groups. It is then repeated on Saturday lunchtime and is immediately followed by its sister programme, *Any Answers?*, where the presenter takes listeners' phone calls, e-mails and faxes in response to issues raised in *Any Questions?*

To represent local radio we selected the *Lesley Riddoch* show, a lunchtime news and discussion programme broadcast on BBC Radio Scotland. The programme lasts for two hours and includes regular news updates, and two or three discussions on topical political and social issues. Public participation is a central feature of the programme and the producers actively encourage public contributions on the telephone or via e-mail. As the programme's website states:

> This is the news and this is your chance to be included in it. Pick up the phone. Send an e-mail. But don't just sit there on the fence, give yourself a voice!

The programme is produced from the main BBC Scotland studios in Glasgow, although there are occasional editions from regional and international locations.

Self-styled as 'the nation's conversation' and the 'most provocative topical phone-in programme', the *Nicky Campbell* Show ran from 9 am to 12 noon on BBC Radio Five Live until January 2003.[10] Although public contributions via phone and e-mail are encouraged throughout the programme, the main phone-in takes place in the first hour, with a summary of the arguments made by participants after the 10 am news. The programme is produced from BBC Television Centre in London, although there are occasional outside broadcasts from regional and international locations.

## The Television Programmes

Three access strands on television were selected.

*Question Time* began in 1979 under the stewardship of Sir Robin Day and was closely modelled on *Any Questions?* It quickly attained status as one of the BBC's flagship political programmes, and involves topical debate of political issues in front of a panel of specially-invited politicians and a studio audience, selected to represent a rough cross-section of the UK public. The programme has undergone a number of changes since 1979, such as the addition of a fifth lay member to the panel (ie, someone who is not a professional politician). At the time of our research *Question Time* was chaired by David Dimbleby, and produced by the independent production company, Mentorn, Barraclough and Carey. The programme is broadcast 'as live' (unedited and approximately one hour after production has finished) on a Thursday evening at 10.30 pm.

*Jonathan Dimbleby* is broadcast at Sunday lunchtimes on ITV 1. This slot has been the home to other political programmes since the 1970s, including *Weekend World* and *Walden*. The programme's host also conducts BBC Radio 4's *Any Questions?*, but the two programmes are very different. *Jonathan Dimbleby* generally involves a one-to-one interview with a politician after which audience members are invited to ask their questions. The *Jonathan Dimbleby* format was adapted by ITV 1 for a series of special programmes with party leaders prior to the 2001 general election (*Ask the Leader*) and for two *Ask the Prime Minister* specials, broadcast in 1999 and 2000.

Finally, *The Wright Stuff* is produced in Norwich by Anglia TV productions for Channel 5 and is broadcast on weekday mornings. The programme is presented by the tabloid journalist Matthew Wright, and deliberately sets out to tackle issues deemed relevant to a predominately female, younger, working class audience. The programme therefore tackles a range of stories covering 'serious' topics such as law and order and health and education, as well as celebrity gossip. The presenter is joined in the studio by two journalists to discuss the main issues of the day and to review the morning newspapers. Public contributions are encouraged by phone and e-mail, and a studio audience are invited to make comments. The production set continues the tabloid theme, with the programme title emblazoned in 'red-top' newspaper style.

In addition to these established access strands, we also spoke to broadcasters involved in the production of the following programmes: *The People Decide* (also known as the Monarchy debate, ITV 1); *Ask the Prime Minister* (ITV 1); *Trial By Night* (Scottish Television); *Your Call* (Sky News); *The Fat Bob Show* (Scot FM).

## Notes

1    If indeed apathy is a function of complacency, we might expect to see the economic and geopolitical uncertainties caused by the September 11 attacks reflected in higher turnouts at future elections in both the US and the UK, as citizens are obliged to pay closer attention to whose fingers are on the military and economic triggers.

2    The total average audience for the two main news bulletins on BBC1 and ITV dropped from twelve million during the general election campaign of 1997, to eight million in 2001.

3    The *Beyond the Sound Bite* report was published in February 2002, having found that viewers of political broadcasting wanted greater diversity of style and tone, a more personalised, less formal approach to coverage of politics, and greater accessability (Kevill, 2002).

4    See *Journalism and Democracy* (McNair, 2000) for a book-length treatment of this subject. The performance of the political media in the 2001 general election is discussed in McNair, 2002. It is argued here that in so far as the content of political media *has* changed in recent years, many of those changes can be read as intelligible, often desirable journalistic adaptations to a rapidly evolving media environment and political culture. The increased journalistic fascination with spin, for example – the journalism of political process, often dismissed by critics as inferior to the coverage of policy substance – can be viewed as a reflection of the rise of public relations as a technology of political news management. The more intensively politicians have used the techniques of promotional culture in the design and presentation of their messages, the more time journalists have devoted to the deconstruction and demystification of those techniques. This is to be welcomed rather than condemned as a dereliction of the journalist's democratic duty, since the power and influence of public relations on political behaviour and action depends largely on its not being recognised by media audiences as contrived artifice.

The journalism of personality and sleaze, on the other hand, expresses in its unflinching intimacy a general decline in the deference traditionally shown to political elites by journalists and public alike; again welcome in so far as deference was often exploited by the powerful in their abuse of office. When deployed with the usual qualifications as to truth, objectivity and balance, it can provide the public with relevant information about political elites.

5    See *Consenting Adults?* (Hibberd, McNair, Schlesinger et al, 2000).

6    Putnam himself concedes that some forms of media consumption – newspaper readership in particular – are positively associated with 'good citizenship', as he defines it. Television watching, however, is blamed by him for the epidemic of civic disengagement seen in America since the 1970s, despite the fact, cited in *Bowling Alone*, that 'Americans who follow news on TV are more knowledgeable about public affairs, vote more regularly, and are generally more active in community affairs' (2000, p.220).

7    From comments made at the symposium on broadcasting and access held by the authors at Stirling University in January 2002.

8   From comments made at the symposium on broadcasting and access held by the authors at Stirling University in January 2002.

9   The first clip lasted seven minutes and was taken from *Question Time*. It featured discussion of the proposed repeal of laws banning the promotion of homosexuality in Scotland. The debate was principally between one advocate for repeal, the singer and gay-rights activist Boy George, and one opponent, the Scottish businessman Brian Souter. The second extract lasted six minutes and was taken from *The Nation Decides* (commonly known as the monarchy debate), broadcast in February 1997. The clip features a raucous debate between pro and anti-monarchists. The third clip lasted seven minutes and was taken from the radio programme, *Any Questions?* and features a debate on law and order. Finally, the fourth clip lasted four minutes and was taken from the *Nicky Campbell* radio programme. The edition selected discussed the environment.

10  Five Live's morning programme is now presented by Fi Glover.

# 2

# Public Participation Broadcasting: A History

Over the past three decades there has been a rapid rise in the number of radio and television programmes to which ordinary members of the public contribute in a participatory capacity. Whether as participants in a radio phone-in or guests in a daytime talk show, their contributions have become a regular part of the UK's programming diet. Appearing on television or radio is no longer restricted to the small group of privileged professionals who once dominated the medium. But the phenomenon of public participation broadcasting is not a new one, and indeed goes back to the earliest days of radio.

This chapter provides a brief overview to the history of public participation in political programming in the UK. Until the 1960s there was comparatively little three-way interaction between broadcasters, politicians and the general public. Political broadcasting tended to be a one-way form of communication with the public receiving news of political developments and events, and hearing the arguments of the respective political parties without the opportunity to question or query political opinions. The policy of excluding the public from taking part in radio or television debates changed markedly in the 1960s, when broadcasters introduced new access formats that heralded the development of public participation in political programmes. This chapter outlines these changes and explains the broad social and industry developments that facilitated them.

## Public service broadcasting in the UK

There are few activities as private as viewing the television set or listening to the radio in the comfort of one's own home. Even programmes aimed at a 'general public' will sometimes be viewed either in isolation or without soliciting any general comment. Before the advent of radio and television broadcasting public life was often confined to open spaces or buildings where people could meet and associate: parks, squares, and promenades, or confined spaces like pubs, cafes, clubs and libraries. Such spaces were also used to seek out information, social instruction or self-improvement. Public events were also directed, much as they are today, towards a particular public in a specific place. Although such events were open to all, they usually appealed to those with particular tastes and needs.

Early broadcasting broke with this model, offering a new type of public forum that offered the potential of including a general public rather than particular segments of it. As Paddy Scannell argues, 'the fundamentally democratic thrust of broadcasting lay in the new kind of access to virtually the whole spectrum of public life ... made available to all' (1989, p.40).

In order to understand how public participation developed in the early years of broadcasting, it is important to understand the philosophy underpinning its organisation in the UK. The concept of public service broadcasting is closely linked with John Reith who, between 1922 and 1936, was the BBC's first General Manager and Director-General. Reith's writings included the first mission statement for public service broadcasters: *Broadcasting Over Britain*, written in 1924.

There were two basic ideas that shaped and informed Reith's management of the BBC (Scannell and Cardiff, 1982, p.163). The first was the belief that a public service broadcaster should be a wholly public-owned entity but politically independent from the state. Reith stated his opposition to direct state control in an uncompromising manner: 'The BBC should be a public service not only in performance but in constitution – but certainly not as a department of state' (Reith, 1949, p.102; Briggs, 1961, pp.235-236). In declaring his forthright opposition to state intervention, Reith was restating the basic premise of liberal thinking: the essential mistrust of state power and the classic liberal doctrine of the media as the Fourth Estate carrying out its 'watchdog function' (Curran, 1991, p.29).

Reith also believed that broadcasting should be independent of any direct commercial pressures. As general manager of the privately-owned British Broadcasting Company (1922-1926), Reith took the extraordinary step of telling the Government-appointed Crawford Committee that broadcasting should be placed under the aegis of a publicly-owned company: 'the trade directors of the BBC knew my views; they had seen the rationality of the argument; had given me leave to speak my mind' (Reith,1949, p.101). Reith had the advantage of seeing the problems facing the wholly commercial American system. Reith was not anti-commercial; his record of leading both public and private companies during his long career bears this out. Instead, he grasped the wider cultural and political importance of broadcasting. It was this idea, of exploring broadcasting's wider pedagogic potential which appealed to him:

> That broadcasting was a potential influence, national and international, of the highest import. That it would have been a prostitution of its worth had the services been used solely for entertainment in the narrow sense. That the informative and educational possibilities must be recognised and developed (ibid., pp.99-100).

In actively lobbying for a publicly-funded broadcasting corporation which was democratically accountable but remained independent of state and big business Reith was explicitly seeking a third way between state and private management of important utilities. In outlining this philosophy of political and market independence Reith demonstrated a remarkable foresight in envisaging new forms of experimental ownership that was an 'outstanding example of the potentiality of a combination of private enterprise and of public control' (Briggs, 1961, p.237). The position adopted by Reith was closer to the concept of the (Habermasian) public sphere than to classic liberal doctrines (Habermas, 1989, pp14-23).[1]

Reith's second idea was that a public service should provide cultural enlightenment; that it should educate and entertain 'by providing everything that is best in every human department of knowledge, endeavour and achievement; and to avoid whatever was or might be hurtful' (Reith, 1949, p.101). Here, Reith is clearly associating himself with the nineteenth century idea of culture as 'a general habit or state of mind', denoting the ideal of human perfection, and the related concept of culture as 'the general state of intellectual development'. This, in late twentieth century terminology, would be seen as a classic statement in favour of high culture as opposed to popular or 'mass culture' (Williams, 1959, pp.xvi-xx). As Reith characteristically added: 'In its earliest years accused of setting out to give the public not what it wanted but what the BBC thought it should have, the answer was that few knew what they wanted, fewer knew what they needed' (1949, p.101). Reith's tight grip meant that the BBC was viewed as a cultural dictatorship, which acted as the arbiter and definer of national tastes and standards. Today, this idea runs contrary to the central tenets of a pluralistic media system.

Reith also believed that broadcasting should have a primary role in promoting the cultural and political values required for the smooth democratic functioning of the country. Certainly, it is not difficult to see what Reith's own cultural preferences were. While Reith trenchantly advocated that the radio system should promote a wide range of values, his policy as director general was one of rigid centralised control, exercised over a unitary system of broadcasting rather than a regionalised one.

Yet there was also a more clearly marked egalitarian side to Reith's thinking. Reith himself argued that:

> Sooner or later broadcasting would cross all paths and be recognised for what it was. That all and sundry, without let or hindrance, might enjoy the interests and diversions hitherto reserved for those with the twin keys of fortune – leisure and money; no home, however favoured, into which some new interests and pleasures might not be introduced (ibid., p.100).

This egalitarianism formed a key component of the Reithian model of public service broadcasting. One of the ways in which Reith sought to provide for the whole public was through his creation of a universal service. This encompassed making provisions for radio (and, later, TV) transmitters to be placed in rural and other outlying areas, the costs of which were high. The BBC was able to achieve this through the availability of a secure source of funding. Access to a guaranteed income through the licence fee allowed the corporation to prioritise in line with its own public service criteria. In being able to create a framework within which to offer a potential service to all, therefore promoting the idea of a common radio service, why should Reith seek to alienate a mass audience through elitist programming? And yet, this is precisely what Reith's BBC helped to achieve, if one considers the extent of public involvement in political broadcasting in its early years.

## Public participation broadcasting: the early years

Until the 1960s the relationship between the BBC and its audience was largely one-way, especially in the provision of news and political programming. The broadcasting of politics was a one-sided affair, with the public receiving news of political developments and events. There was little, if any, chance for the public to interrogate political elites. Neither the BBC nor the political parties encouraged such interaction. In the early years of the BBC, therefore, public contributions to programming remained limited. As the broadcasting historian Paddy Scannell has argued:

> You will find that in the first three or four years of BBC radio there were request programmes and people were interviewed in the studio. There is some evidence that there were, at least, phone-in request programmes, although I'm not certain there were such things as phone-in talk programmes. The idea of making ordinary listeners or audience members active participants on radio was there from the beginning and it was something the BBC deliberately turned away from when it became a national broadcasting institution in 1927.[2]

This was due, in part, to the growth and development of national and regional output and the closure of local stations. But antipathy towards public involvement in broadcasting was also due to class and professional biases among BBC staff, beginning with Reith himself:

> In some stations, I see, periodically, men down to speak whose status either socially or professionally, and whose qualifications to speak, seem doubtful. It should be an honour, in every sense of the word, for a man to speak from any broadcasting station. And only those who have a claim to be heard above their fellows on any particular subject in the locality should be put on these programmes.[3]

In this respect, Reith was a man of his time, and his statement should not be taken in isolation from recognition of his more egalitarian efforts. In key areas of national policy, Reith was keen to nurture limited public participation (if without the involvement of politicians), even when this caused political storm. In the Talks Department, for example, producers took a more 'progressive' approach to public involvement in radio programmes. In 1934 one series, *Time to Spare*, examined the consequences of unemployment, inviting ordinary working-class people to discuss the harsh consequences of mass unemployment and life on the dole. Eleven people spoke in total, including a miner and a homeless person. The scheduling of this programme coincided with the final parliamentary stages of a new Unemployment Bill, with testimonies from *Time to Spare* being used by Labour MPs in speeches seeking to strengthen unemployment benefit (Scannell and Cardiff, 1991, p.65).

Unsurprisingly, perhaps, the government was incensed by BBC interference at a time of high social unrest. The Cabinet thought about stopping the series and the then Prime Minister, Ramsey MacDonald, summoned Reith to Downing Street to request that the talks be stopped. Reith's reply to MacDonald – as retold by the programme's producer, Felix Greene, to Scannell and Cardiff – was:

> That it was within the power of the government to order the BBC to discontinue the series but that if it did he would, at that time in the schedule when the talks should be given, instruct the announcer to declare that the next twenty minutes would be silent because the Government had refused to allow the unemployed to express their views (1991, p.66).

MacDonald backed down and the series continued. Reluctant as Reith was to use public service broadcasting as a forum of debate between the public and their elected representatives, there was even more reluctance on behalf of political elites to open themselves up via broadcasting to greater public scrutiny. Politicians, where possible, strictly resisted broadcaster interference in their affairs and defended the primacy of parliament as the forum for national debate. This last point is best illustrated by the development in 1943 of a new kind of 'audience participation' programme, *Everybody's Mike*. The programme, produced by Howard Thomas (who had already enjoyed enormous success with *The Brains Trust* and would later produce *Any Questions?*),[4] involved six MPs answering questions put to them by the comedian Naughton Wayne, but sent by members of the public. The MPs, anticipating a light-hearted factual programme similar to *The Brains Trust*, refused to take part when they were told of the programme's format. Quintin Hogg, appointed Lord Chancellor in Margaret Thatcher's government, wrote:

> Although most Members of Parliament are anxious to get in touch with people and not in the least anxious to stand on their dignity, there is a point at which it becomes highly improper for them to allow themselves to be guyed innocently or intentionally … It rests with all bodies responsible for the dissemination of information, to treat our democratic institutions with a certain amount of respect, and the fact that in this case no disrespect was intended in some ways constitutes an aggravation and not an excuse, because it shows, on the part of those responsible for the programme, a complete failure to understand the nature of our constitution (quoted in Briggs, 1970, p.620).

Indeed, BBC managers agreed with Hogg, stating that:

> The House of Commons is the greatest democratic institution in the world, and the BBC has a clear and obvious duty to democracy in general

and to democracy in this country in particular to present the House of Commons (and this of course includes all its members) to listeners only in such a way as is consistent with its true position, dignity and importance (ibid., pp. 620-21).

Public participation in political programmes was thus prevented in the early years of broadcasting by a formidable alliance of the BBC and political elites. The BBC only began to reverse this policy in the post-1945 period, when tentative moves were made to encourage greater public participation in radio programming, including political formats. It took some politicians even longer to accept the idea that the public could play an important part in mediated political discussion. In our current research, we still found politicians with trenchant views against public access programmes that, in their words, 'don't get to the heart of the issues' (see chapter five).

## Public participation broadcasting in postwar Britain

Asa Briggs has argued that without the interruption of the war commercial broadcasting would have been introduced fifteen years earlier than it eventually was, in 1955. Certainly, the political, economic and social climate that greeted the development of radio and television services in 1947 was very different from that of 1939. The BBC itself realised that it needed to take a leading part in the period of reconstruction to strengthen democratic ideas (Briggs, 1970, p.715). Public service broadcasting was identified as one of the main institutions which could help promote the three postwar strategies of western European states: reconciliation, which required selective amnesia of past events; promotion of 'founding myths' for hope and renewal; and enactment of state-led policy measures to encourage greater political, social and economic equity (Judt, 1994, pp. 2-4).

There were, however, increasing commercial pressures which threatened the BBC's monopoly as Britain's public service broadcaster. From the 1920s to the late 1940s businesses were unwilling to invest in the television and radio broadcasting business. By the early 1950s, however, they had scented the beginning of a consumer society and guessed the profits to be made from television advertising. A new commercial lobby demanding an end to the BBC's broadcasting monopoly quickly found supporters in the Conservative party. Supporters of commercial television were not helped by the Beveridge Committee, set up by the Labour government in 1947 to examine the future of broadcasting policy when the BBC's Charter expired in 1955. The Committee took detailed evidence from all sides of the debate and while it noted the opinion of the pro-commercial lobby the final Report argued that if broadcasting were to maintain its social functions, it had to be protected from commercial pressures. But while the committee protected public service broadcasting it was also highly critical of the BBC, 'beginning with Londonisation, going on to secretiveness and self-satisfaction and ending up with a dangerous sense of mission which had become a sense of divine right' (Curran and Seaton, 1997, p. 162). But the Beveridge Committee was not united in its findings and one member, the Conservative politician Selwyn Lloyd, produced his own report that advocated the cause of commercial broadcasting. Lloyd's report was important because the Conservative Party adopted his arguments as official party policy before the 1951 General Election, an election they subsequently won.

The Beveridge Report was published in the final year of the Labour Government. Despite that government's acceptance of Beveridge's main recommendations, and its rejection of the minority report, the incoming Conservative government quickly set about enacting Selwyn Lloyd's plans. In 1952 the government introduced proposals to establish commercial television. The news of these proposals provoked intense political debate on behalf of supporters of both sides of the argument. In support of the BBC's monopoly John (now Lord) Reith compared the introduction of commercial broadcasting to smallpox, the bubonic plague and the Black Death. But Reith's views were in the minority (Smith, 1974). The legislation for commercial television was formally introduced in Parliament in 1953 and became law in 1954.

Against this background the BBC undertook to develop and strengthen its political coverage, although until ITV started broadcasting in 1955 the BBC dragged its feet in introducing new and innovative ways of presenting politics on TV and radio. Change was slow in coming, and Briggs states that the BBC 'was never anxious between 1945 and 1955 to get deeply entangled in politics as presenter of the news or as an organizer of a forum of argument' (1979, p.615). The opportunities afforded to the public to participate in broadcast debates remained limited.

The BBC restricted active public involvement to a limited number of programmes, including the political access programme, *Any Questions?*, which began in the Western region in 1948. The programme was eventually given a nationwide transmission slot, and continues broadcasting today as the longest-running political access programme on radio. As noted in chapter one, the programme's format reflected the political and social values of 1940s Britain. Public participation was strictly limited only to asking questions, with limited possibility of entering into dialogue with politicians. And political parties signalled their resistance to the programme by refusing for many years to allow senior politicians of Cabinet level to take part in the programme (Day, 1989, p.276). Only later was this rule relaxed and greater public participation also encouraged in the form of *Any Answers?*, a phone-in programme that today follows the Saturday repeat of *Any Questions?*

This situation remained broadly unchanged until the first half of the 1960s, when television and radio broadcasters, led by the BBC, began to develop styles and formats of programming where members of the public gained a higher degree of visibility. This increase was due in part to the overall expansion in the BBC's radio and television political coverage. But it was also due, as Sylvia Harvey argues, to 'a new spirit of democratisation' that developed in the 1960s and which saw the erosion of deference and Reithian paternalism, and 'the emergence of more egalitarian patterns of thought' (2000, p.161). By the 1960s social conditions were evolving fast and the decade saw massive political upheavals across Europe. People, on the whole, were healthier and better educated. Economic growth had also led to significant increases in living standards. In many ways the public had matured, especially in their broadcasting tastes.

The rapid success of ITV (highlighted by the rise in TV sets in the UK from one million in 1951 to thirteen million by 1964) and the periodic review of the BBC's Charter led the Macmillan government in 1960 to set up a new committee, chaired by Sir Henry Pilkington, to examine the structure and organisation of television in the UK. The Pilkington Report was published in 1962 and immediately caused a political storm. The committee was highly critical of commercial broadcasting, arguing that its introduction had undermined programme standards. The main fear expressed by the committee was that the continuation of commercial broadcasting in its (then) present form would lead to the 'permanent degradation' of content (Smith, 1974, p.126). Although the BBC had a strong tradition of public service the committee argued that the advent of commercial television had inevitably led to competition for audiences and to programming that attracted the lowest common denominator. For many members of the Pilkington committee the arrival of commercial television threatened the cohesion of the viewing public, with the explicit fear being that this would cause social fragmentation (especially among the working classes). While the Conservative government rejected this argument, the Pilkington Report aided the BBC in so far as the third television channel, when it was set up in 1964, was allocated to the BBC and not to a commercial operator. Clearly, the report played an influential role in the government's decision (Smith, 1974, pp. 126-30).

While it is true that ITV had introduced more populist programme formats, Pilkington's pessimistic warning was clearly flawed and, with hindsight, an early example of the rhetoric of 'dumbing down' which accompanies almost every effort to reform and innovate political broadcasting to this day (see below). In fact, the emergence of ITV as a competitor to the BBC incentivised the latter to be more adventurous, if still as a public service broadcaster. Anthony Smith argues that:

> Producers within the BBC were more often conscious of an internal competition between different sections of the BBC, producing an enormous flowering of talent and inventiveness, which became characteristic of broadcasting in the first half of the 1960s; the coming of commercial television had undoubtedly produced a mood of competitiveness, but the changes which occurred within the BBC were not to any great extent imitative of independent television. The BBC pioneered daring forms of television satire, it instituted professionalised political interviewing, and adopted traditional journalistic standards in its current affairs programmes. ITV for much of the time found itself lagging slightly behind the BBC in viewing figures, but its journalistic work too became confident and highly professionalised (ibid., p.130).

And, indeed, it was the BBC not ITV which introduced many of the access formats that, from the 1960s onwards would seek, albeit imperfectly, to represent the new spirit of democratisation. The first of these programmes, *Election Forum*, was a television programme where viewers' questions were put to senior politicians immediately prior to the 1964 election campaign. But while this programme introduced a limited form of audience participation, it still had major shortcomings. As the programme's co-presenter, Robin Day, later argued:

> It did not have real audience participation by visible voters in the flesh ...
> Nor did *Election Forum* offer independent probing by professional
> interviewers who could be relied upon to ask, and to follow up, relevant
> and up-to-minute election questions. The most serious shortcoming of
> *Election Forum* was that all three programmes went out before the
> dissolution, in other words before the campaign was under way. The
> voters' questions could not deal with the issues as they had developed
> during the campaign (Day, 1989, p.182).

The 1960s also saw the emergence of a new programme format that soon became a firm favourite with broadcasters: the radio phone-in programme. The first radio phone-in shows were developed in United States in the 1950s. With the development of phone-in programmes members of the public were on a routine basis actively encouraged to contribute to issues under discussion in the studio, including political and social debates. With the commencement of BBC local radio in 1967 phone-in formats were developed in many areas including Leicester, Nottingham and Sheffield, although for many programme makers the first attempts to organise radio phone-in programmes were less than successful. The British public were still largely unaccustomed to requests for their views and, unsurprisingly, the quality of debate was often poor. The advent of commercial local radio in 1973 led to a further expansion of phone-in programmes. For these stations, the phone-in was seen as an ideal programme format, combining as it did genuine popular appeal with relatively low production costs.

Local phone-in programmes were soon adapted into national radio formats, including, in 1970, the start of a new political show, *It's Your Line* with Robin Day. This was followed in 1974 by the start of *Election Call*, where leading political figures were questioned on a range of issues during the (two) election campaigns that year. In his book on the February 1974 election, David Butler argued,

> It attracted over a million listeners, and up to 9000 calls. It was chaired
> with exemplary skill and fairness by Robin Day. The public's questions
> were often penetrating and sometimes blunter than any professional
> questioner would dare to be ... Clearly a campaign tradition has been
> born (Quoted in Day, 1989, p.184).

The breakdown in negotiations between the BBC and popular presenter Michael Parkinson to host a new late night chat show left a gap in its schedule for autumn 1979. To help fill that gap, the BBC adapted the popular radio programme, *Any Questions?*, to a weekly television programme, *Question Time*, originally hosted by the ever-present Robin Day, and presented as of this writing by David Dimbleby. From the outset, *Question Time* producers sought to differentiate the programme from its radio cousin. While the number of panel members remained the same (four), producers encouraged greater audience participation and the programme was made longer (60 minutes, as against the original length of 45). *Question Time* soon proved a popular addition to the late-night schedule, although few anticipated this at the outset:

> The title *Question Time* had been chosen because no one could think of anything better ... But no one bothered too much about the title because no one thought the programme would last very long (Day, 1989, p.276).

The programme has subsequently been developed and refined, with the addition of a fifth panelist and an enhanced role for audience members (see chapter five).

In commercial television, too, public access forms have increased in popularity in the past three decades, albeit largely in non-peak time slots. ITV's traditional Sunday lunchtime political slot, which started with *Weekend World* in the 1970s, has now become a public access programme (*Jonathan Dimbleby*).

New TV channels have also developed access formats as part of their political coverage. Channel 4 (which began transmission in 1982) has experimented with a number of access programmes, including its *On Trial ...* series and *The People's Parliament*, presented by Sheena MacDonald in the 1990s. More recently Channel 4 has staged broadcast debates chaired by *C4 News* presenter Jon Snow on single issue topics such as the health service and the conflict in the Middle East. In the latter, broadcast in October 2002, viewers were invited to contribute opinions as to whether a possible war with Iraq was, (a) inevitable, and (b) desirable (BBC 1 also organised a debate on this topic, broadcast around the same time – both provided access to views which were highly critical of UK government policy on Iraq).

Since its launch in 1997 (and despite having a less rigorous public service remit than the other four terrestrial channels) Channel 5 has broadcast a number of public participation programmes, including one strand presented by Kirsty Young addressing issues such as the legalisation of soft drugs. Channel 5 also launched a morning audience and phone-in programme, *The Wright Stuff*, which frequently addresses political themes. SkyNews has *Your Call* and other access programmes presented by its political editor, Adam Boulton.[5]

On radio, there has been a rise in the numbers of political access programmes on air, associated with the dramatic growth in speech radio (although there have been signs in the past few years that demand has peaked, at least in the commercial sector). As the number of national and local radio channels has increased in the last two decades, so has the space available for talk radio. Indeed, as was noted earlier, talk radio is a particularly cost effective way of filling the countless hours of airtime which now comprise the UK radio sector. For the BBC a key moment in this process was the launch of Radio Five Live in March 1994, a station wholly devoted to news and sport. Five Live has weekday morning and late evening phone-in programmes tackling major political and social issues such as the *Nicky Campbell* show, but all its news programmes encourage listener participation via e-mail or text messaging. The station has also developed new sports discussion programmes in the mould of political access formats, including *Any Sporting Questions?*, based on *Any Questions?*, and *606*, the sports phone-in programme. The first (national) commercial radio station devoted wholly to speech, Talk Radio, increased the amount of political access programming with phone-ins presented by such as Brian Hayes (its demise in 1999, to become Talk Sport, highlights the growing popularity of sports discussion programmes in recent years).[6]

Broadcasters have also increased the amount of public participation in conventional news and current affairs programmes, by inviting audiences to comment on the major political issues. Today, many radio and television news programmes include regular slots to read out audience letters, faxes and phone. Such feedback has been further encouraged with the development of new technologies such as e-mails and message boards (see chapter six). Some programmes have sought to encourage public participation at election times by broadcasting special editions with live audiences.

## Conclusion

Since the late 1940s, though not without some resistance, as we have seen, public participation in political programming has been one of the strategies by which broadcasters have sought to persuade and reassure the listening or viewing audience that their services are relevant to the lives and concerns of ordinary people. Phone-in shows and audience discussion programmes have become a permanent feature of radio and TV schedules in the UK, offering viewers the opportunity to see themselves, or others like them, apparently holding their own in the company of resident presenters and guests. As noted in chapter one, recent studies into the 'crisis' of political broadcasting suggest that they remain an important tool for mobilising and engaging audiences (Kevill, 2002; Hargreaves and Thomas, 2002). The rest of this book examines the construction of access programming, and assesses the contribution it makes to the health of Britain's political public sphere, and ultimately to the democratic process itself.

## Notes

1    The term public sphere is intimately linked to the rise of the liberal state. The liberal state was founded upon the basic or inviolable rights accorded to male property owners. It was as a result of these new found rights and the extension of the political franchise to the emerging property owning class that new public institutions were founded within civil society. The growth of newspapers, libraries, universities and debating societies in turn led to the formation of a new form of political power, public opinion. And the growth of public opinion inevitably reconfigured the nature and shape of political debate. The formation of these institutions collectively represented a public sphere. For Habermas, the characteristics of this new political space included: protection from traditional public authorities, the Church and the state; and the accessibility of the new institutions due to their low operating costs. Such a public sphere promoted a whole series of debates as to the nature and direction

of society. The rational nature of this debate, in line with the wider beliefs of the Enlightenment movement, emphasised human progress in all spheres of life.

2    Quoted in 'You're on the Air', broadcast by BBC Radio 4, February 2001.

3    Quoted in 'You're on the Air', broadcast by BBC Radio 4, February 2001.

4    The provisional title for *The Brains Trust* was *Any Questions* (note the missing question mark, which distinguishes its title from that of the popular Radio 4 access programme). *The Brains Trust* consisted of key celebrities, including politicians, answering factual questions from the members of the general public, and led to the formation of general knowledge clubs being set up around the country.

5    Channel 4 was set up as a direct response to the 1977 report of the government-appointed Annan Committee. While the committee was somewhat sceptical about the potential of access programming in general, it did argue for 'the open expression of a wide range of views from many different groups', while endorsing the view that 'the basic principle of access programming is freedom to state opinions' (Home Office, 1977: 296, quoted from Harvey, 2000: 162).

6    According to John Lloyd, Head of News and Current Affairs, the popularity of political access programmes might have peaked in the early 1990s, and there is now less appetite among some commercial broadcasters for political access programmes (Interview with authors, 2001). The build up to war with Iraq in late 2002/2003, however, showed that access broadcasting remains an important element in the construction of national public debate on key political issues.

# 3

# Constructing Access, I:
# Representation

That citizens should have a degree of access to those who govern their lives, and some level of participation in the processes by which political decisions are made, are essential characteristics of a healthy democracy. The exercise of political power in a democracy is, after all, undertaken on behalf of the people. If politicians are to be accountable to those who elect them into office the latter, logic dictates, must have access to, and be able to participate in, the processes by which power is acquired and exercised. At the most fundamental level, this means the widest possible access to formal democratic participation – specifically, the right to vote. This right has in the course of two centuries or so, if not without often bitter struggle, gradually been extended to all British adults regardless of their socio-economic status, sex, ethnicity, or educational attainment.

But if that right is to be worth having, the voter must also have access to accurate and truthful information about public affairs, so that he or she is able to make rational choices between the competing political programmes which democratic elections exist to test. It is this requirement for reliable, objective information which defines the role of the media in normative democratic theory. It puts on journalists the responsibility to report political events accurately and, where it is warranted, critically; to interpret those events, making sense of their complexity within prescribed rules of objectivity and balance (in the UK, for example, impartiality rules impose strict limits on the broadcasters' freedom to interpret events, while press editors are permitted to be partisan, though pluralistic and diverse across the print sector as a whole); and to provide a platform for competing parties, from which they can disseminate their messages to their potential voters (as in party political broadcasts, or in columns written for a newspaper).

To assist them in evaluating this information citizens in a democracy require access to spaces in which they can speak and discuss their political views publicly, without fear or favour, and not only when it is time to cast their votes but between elections, as a matter of routine. They should, as Chambers and Costain (2000) note, be able to pass critical comment on their governors, and expect their voices to be heard. William Gamson writes that 'public discourse can and should empower citizens, give them voice and agency, build community, and help citizens to act on behalf of their interests and values. The normative standard here is one of engaging citizens in the democratic process through their active participation in the public sphere' (2001, pp.56-71).

The main vehicles for the exercise of such participation have always been, and are today more than ever, the media. From the first readers' letters published by newspapers in the seventeenth century to e-mail or text messaging participation in the radio and television programmes of the twenty first, the facilitation of public access to political debate has been recognised as an important democratic function of the journalistic 'fourth estate'. As key agents of public discourse the media in their coverage of political affairs facilitate democracy by furnishing citizens with knowledge, and by giving them both motive and opportunity to contribute to the processes of policy making and governance. Stephen Coleman argues that in a democracy 'there must exist channels of communication providing for a free flow of information both amongst citizens and between representatives and voters' (1999, p.67). L. F. Rakow emphasises the democratic importance of a "citizen-based communication system"(1999, p. 79). Where straight journalism provides the information (in the form of news and commentary) on which a deliberative democracy is founded, access media exist to provide opportunities for public participation in political discourse, both as a means by which citizens acquire political information (by reading or listening to the views of others in letters and debates, for example), and as a prelude or incentive to political action, whether that be voting in an election or taking part in a demonstration. In specific terms the media of public participation provide access to:

(i) debating fora in which individual and public opinions about political issues can be formed, and;

(ii) members of political elites, in contexts where they are obliged to engage in debate with ordinary citizens.

## The forms of access

In practical terms, mediated political participation will take one of two forms: actual contributions to the media which make up the public sphere, such as readers' letters or telephone calls to radio and TV talk shows; or membership of the various spectating communities – audiences – who access those contributions indirectly, and are thus enabled to utilise them in the formation of their own political ideas and opinions. The writing and reading of reader's letters to newspapers and periodicals are the oldest forms of such participation, as old as the print media themselves.[1] Audiences for access broadcasting, however – especially those on the main UK networks – cut across the readerships of many newspapers, allowing them to act as national, UK-wide debating fora in a way that newspapers cannot. Where British newspapers are permitted (indeed, expected) to be partisan in their editorial viewpoints, broadcast media are legally required to avoid party political bias, and thus tend to draw their audiences from across the ideological spectrum. They are also trusted to a greater degree. At the start of the 2001 general election research commissioned by ITN found that 77 per cent trusted the BBC as a news source, 74 per cent trusted ITN, and only 41 per cent trusted newspapers.[2] The status and authority of British public service broadcasting is one reason why the leading access programmes regularly have more impact on political debate, as indicators of public opinion, than even the most widely read newspapers.

The forms of broadcast access vary from medium to medium and channel to channel, in what is a mixed media economy and an increasingly fragmented market of niche audiences. The main types found in the British media are:

- *the studio debate*, where an audience drawn from the public at large is invited to put questions to a panel of politicians and/or appropriately qualified experts, usually comprising four or more individuals. The form is represented in this study by *Any Questions?* and *Question Time* (BBC radio and TV respectively). The questions debated on these programmes tend to be news-driven, reflecting what participants and programme producers feel to be at the top of the political agenda at any given time. On occasion the expert panel may be replaced by a single, senior politician, up to the level of the prime minister, as in the run-up to the 1997 and 2001 general elections, when *Question Time* featured access to each of the main party leaders;

- the *phone-in debate*, on radio and (less commonly) TV, in which callers contribute to studio discussion, or put questions to politicians and other experts over the line. Issue-led and news-driven, the phone-in show tends to focus on one or two issues over a two or three-hour period, allowing for prolonged debate. Programme makers select the subjects for debate based on their professional assessments of what is newsworthy and topical. The format is represented in this study by two BBC productions (the *Nicky Campbell* and *Lesley Riddoch* programmes), and one on the local commercial station, Scot FM (*The Fat Bob Show*);[3]

- the *single-issue debate*, in which members of the public are invited to decide the merits of a single issue by listening to the presentation of competing views (which may include the views of the audience). Such debates may be immediately topical, like the one-off debates on the health service and education organised by the BBC and Channel 4 in the run-up to the 2001 general election.[4] Or, as in the case of *The Nation Decides* on ITV in 1997 (the monarchy debate), they may have a less overt connection with the short-term news agenda. The BBC's *You Decide*, chaired by senior journalist Jeremy Paxman for the duration of its short life, tackled such topics as the legalisation of cannabis and gun control – on the political agenda, certainly, but not necessarily in the news when the programmes were transmitted. In late 2002, as tension mounted between Britain, the USA and Iraq over the issue of weapons of mass destruction, BBC 1 and Channel 4 both ran one-off access specials on the merits or otherwise of going to war.

Some programmes combine more than one of these elements (studio debate and phone-in, for example), or mix access with more traditional journalistic mechanisms such as the one-on-one political interview (as in the *Jonathan Dimbleby* show).

## The aims of access

Formal differences aside, political access programmes as we define them here all involve some element of *public participation*, organised for the purpose of achieving three goals (in addition to the basic function, shared with other journalistic media, of providing political information to the audience) in support of the democratic process. These can be characterised as:

- *representation* of the people in the public sphere;

- *interrogation* – what Habermas (1989) has called the *critical scrutiny* of, or *critical publicity* towards – political elites by the people;

- the *mobilisation* of citizens to participate in politics, whether that involvement takes the form of voting or some other mode of participation, such as party membership, involvement in single issue campaigning, or simply thinking in a sustained way about politics. In the terms frequently heard in current debates about the crisis of democratic participation, this aim can also be defined as *engagement* of citizens in the political process. Through engagement in the issues addressed by access programmes, individuals may be mobilised to take part, at some level, in the democratic processes through which issues are resolved (a lobby of the House of Commons, for example).

These are the *normative* aspirations of political access programming; the democratic goals which programme-makers set for themselves, and against which their effectiveness as mechanisms of mediated democratic participation will be evaluated here.

Chapter two described how British access programming developed against the background of resource constraints caused by an ever-more competitive media environment in which airtime for political broadcasting tends to become scarcer; the consequent necessity for producers to take into account the aesthetics of good programme-making; and a changing political culture in which the nature of 'the public', and the expectations of that public in respect of their interaction with political elites, have significantly altered in the half century or so since the birth of public participation broadcasting in Britain. Our focus in this and the next chapter is on the perspectives of programme makers on these issues; their views on what contribution access broadcasting should and can make to the facilitation of democratic participation; and how, within the above constraints, they have sought to construct it within individual programmes.

## Representing the public

The idea of representation is of course fundamental to democracy, and from the birth of the access genre in the late 1940s has been a key structuring element in the design of public participation programming. Representation in this context refers both to the programmes' status as indices of the balance of political and public opinion in the country, and to their constitution of the public in the public sphere, in all its social and demographic complexity.

In so far as they aspire to be representative access programmes aim to function as visible symbols of 'people power'. The displays of mediated public participation which they allow are visible signifiers of democracy itself, in the same way that the rituals observed at the state opening of parliament are intended to signify the constitutional subordination of the monarchy to the commons. Access programmes on radio and television represent the people to themselves, in the process of engaging with the political elite. They give the people voice, real and symbolic, as a support to the exercise of their democratic power.

To have resonance at this ideological (in the Barthesian sense) level the demographic composition of participating members of the public must be accepted by audiences as a representative sampling of 'the people', and their views as expressed on air as a valid indicator of what 'the people' are thinking about current political issues. Success in achieving this quality of representativeness gives a programme heightened status in the public sphere, allowing it a role in shaping the journalistic and political agendas. One of the criteria of the effectiveness of access programming often cited by their producers (see below) is the extent to which politicians take note of and act on what it tells them about the state of public opinion. The degree of attention they or their advisers pay to the views expressed by participants is directly related to their perception not just of a particular programme's popularity and audience reach, but its reliability as a barometer of public opinion. This latter is a function of how a programme is made. One of the main production challenges for public participation broadcasters is to ensure that those who gain access to programmes comprise (or are seen by the audience as comprising) a representative sample of the British people.

This challenge has been complicated by the evolution of British political culture in the post-World War II period, driven by changing social attitudes to class, gender, and ethnicity, as well as the onset, post-1997, of devolution and other constitutional reforms set in motion by the Labour government which came to power in that year. Taken together, these processes have undermined the traditional notion of a unitary Great British public, and encouraged some recognition of the UK as a multi-nation state comprising many, often overlapping publics defined by such criteria as social class, gender, ethnicity, nationality, geography and lifestyle. All of these, normative democratic theory would suggest, have the right to, and need for, some representation in the expanded public sphere of the twenty-first century. The broadcasters, as we shall see, profess to understand that need, and to this extent the history of public participation programming in Britain is the history of producers' efforts to expand and refine their socio-demographic reach, and to find modes of facilitating access appropriate to the many different publics they now aspire to serve.

In that process the makers of mediated representation have revised the conception of 'the people' which underpins their work. This evolution can be characterised as a movement from a conception of public participation which can be viewed as broadsheet in content and style (designed for a relatively educated and affluent public), to forms which can be described as mid-market and tabloid (targeted at a less educated, less affluent audience).

## Any Questions?

To observe this process unfold we will begin with the very first example of the public participation genre in the UK – BBC radio's *Any Questions?* which, in its embodiment of an earlier, more deferential model of how access should be organised, shows how far the genre has developed in recent years. Since its establishment in 1948 *Any Questions?* has brought a sample of the public together on most Fridays of the year to question four panelists – typically comprising three professional politicians and one other, such as a journalist, a senior public servant, or a lobbyist, judged competent to comment on political issues. This panel is representative in so far as it contains a balance of political viewpoints from left to right of the parliamentary political spectrum (in the UK this usually means one Labour, one Conservative and one Liberal Democrat member), supplemented on occasion by a panelist drawn from a recognised pressure group such as Friends of the Earth or the Countryside Alliance. Editions of the programme recorded in Scotland, Wales or Northern Ireland will reflect the distinctive political environments to be found in those areas, with representatives from nationalist parties such as the SNP and Plaid Cymru usually included.

The composition of the panel is biased towards constitutional, parliamentary politics, since representativeness is measured mainly in terms of party strength in the House of Commons. In this sense the *Any Questions?* panel is a kind of parliamentary democracy in miniature, both in its reproduction of a symbolic House of Commons, and in its construction of democratic accountability. It is a visible demonstration of the accessibility of the political class to the voting public (represented both in the audience present at the recording, and the larger audience listening to the Radio 4 broadcast at home), and a weekly reminder of their readiness to subject themselves to questioning. Ensuring that they answer the questions adequately is a chairman drawn from the senior ranks of the fourth estate – journalist and documentary-maker Jonathan Dimbleby (Nick Clarke and Robin Lustig stand in for Dimbleby on occasion) – with the authority and the journalistic licence to act as watchdog over them.

The rise of feminism and other forms of identity politics has meant that *Any Questions?* panels (and those of comparable programmes like *Question Time*) must, as far as possible, also be representative in terms of gender and ethnicity. On rare occasions, such as an edition of the show recorded in 2000 attended by the authors, the panel is all-male, to the stated embarrassment of the production team.[5] The producer on this occasion explained that, while there had been editions of *Any Questions?* in which two or even three members of the panel have been women, there are "not as many good female [as male] performers"[6] out there, and tokenism was resisted for aesthetic reasons. Because panelists on this programme, like others, must be not just expert but articulate, stimulating debate by the quality of their contributions as much as the representativeness of their opinions, rigid formulae of class, gender, ethnic or party balance are not applied if they are likely to adversely affect programme quality. The structure of expert participation on access programmes as a whole thus tends to reflect deep-rooted cultural and structural biases (against women in senior positions, for example, which still exist in the UK despite the impact of more than three decades of feminism).

This panel of political experts is then confronted with an audience of about five hundred individuals drawn from the public. Without a full-time audience researcher on the staff, *Any Questions?* relies on its host institution to supply the majority of its studio audience, with guidelines for selection provided by the producers. Schools, universities and other public institutions apply to host the programme on a given week, and the demographic composition of participants is skewed accordingly. An edition of the programme attended by the authors in December 2000 contained a large number of academic psychologists, for example, who were attending their annual conference in Glasgow. Their professional association was acting as host for that week's programme, and supplied much of the audience. In this respect the *Any Questions?* audience is representative less of the people as a whole than a sub-set of what are probably its more civically engaged, politically motivated members – the concerned middle classes, the professions, those who might already be thought more likely to participate in the political process, and can engage with the panelists as active citizens. One participant interviewed for this research observed from his own experience that the *Any Questions?* audience is 'selective'.

> I know people in that audience who are involved in a number of things. I'm on the governing body of a school. I'm chairman of the governors, and some of the people I was sitting with – two or three of them were councillors. There were a couple of councillors in another part of the hall.

The limitations which this approach places on *Any Questions?* representativeness are recognised by the programme's producers, who work on the basis that 'if you go to a private school in Surrey you're going to get five hundred good, interested listeners all packed in', with a listening audience of 'nice middle class families … An elderly audience, I would say, and quite a middle class audience, that's our bedrock'.[7] To this extent *Any Questions?* reflects the political culture of the immediate post-war era when it was established, and when certain assumptions prevailed about who was best qualified to participate in political debate, what it was appropriate for ordinary people to say, and when the still-relatively uneducated working classes (as well as women and ethnic minority groups) were excluded from all but walk-on and vox pop roles in the public sphere. *Any Questions?* came on air at a transitional moment in British democracy, not long after the Second World War when, although the public-politician relationship was opening up, it still embodied much of the deference of pre-war times. While these inhibitions are no longer so dominant across the public sphere as a whole, they still survive in pockets such as *Any Questions?* contemporary Radio 4 audience – 'middle class, and white', as one producer frankly concedes. More than fifty years after its establishment this approach, and the composition of its audience, both in the recording theatre and at home, remind us of an earlier, more innocent era, when asking questions of, and talking back to politicians was deemed a privilege rather than a right of citizenship. Audience members ask their questions and then sit silently as they are answered. Very occasionally, chairman Jonathan Dimbleby will allow a questioner to make a follow up comment – 'I have this sixth sense that they will be able to deliver something, but I only go back if they want to come in again, and if they do they generally have something important to say' – but otherwise the audience are relatively passive.

Despite these limitations – because of them, perhaps – *Any Questions?* enjoys the affection accorded a national treasure, and an audience of around 1.8 million for its two transmissions (the Friday evening broadcast is repeated on a Saturday afternoon). These are large audiences for speech radio, and give the programme a degree of political authority which regularly attracts senior politicians up to the level of Cabinet ministers.

## Expanding Access

In its reasonableness and good humour *Any Questions?* is, for many, a model of how mediated political debate should be conducted in Britain. And yet, as we have seen, its audience is comprised mainly of those who are likely to be relatively well-equipped with cultural capital and already engaged in a range of political processes, from membership of school boards to involvement in single issue campaigns and party work. We point this out not to criticise the programme, which appears to serve its target audience very well, but to suggest that its value as a participatory vehicle does not extend to the many millions of citizens usually implicated in the crisis of democratic participation – the tabloid audience, as it were. Subsequent developments in the political access genre have sought to provide more representative participatory fora, and to target those who are less engaged politically than the typical *Any Questions?* audience; those, in short, who may be lacking in many of the cultural resources usually associated with active citizenship and who might, if access broadcasting can indeed play a role in enhancing political participation, be thought most likely to benefit from it.

The limited representativeness of *Any Questions?* is recognised by its producers, as we have seen, and while its continuing presence in the political public sphere is ensured by the size and assertiveness of its loyal audience, efforts have been made to widen the scope of public participation in its debates. *Any Answers?* allows members of the listening audience to phone in and express their views on that week's *Any Questions?* In contrast to the latter, says one member of the production team, participants in this second tier of access 'actively contribute in a very positive way. They're not constrained, and they've had time to mull it over'.

While the demographic profile of *Any Answers?* phone-in participants still reflects the more elderly, middle class composition of the Radio 4 audience they are drawn from a UK-wide pool of listeners, much larger than the few hundred who make it to a live recording of the programme.

The expansion of broadcast access on television was furthered by the launch of *Question Time*, which premiered on BBC 1 in 1979, and is today the corporation's flagship participation programme. *Question Time* shares some obvious formal characteristics with *Any Questions?*, on which it was modelled. An expert panel made up predominantly of professional politicians takes questions on topical political issues from an invited audience, chaired by a respected journalist (at the time of our research he was David Dimbleby, the brother of Jonathan) – but there are some key differences. To ensure a more representative audience the programme makers select for participation what David Dimbleby describes as a 'fairly crude but quite effective cross section [of the public] based on age and gender, race and political affiliation'.

This is achieved by the presenter's on-air invitation to members of the TV audience to apply to attend future recordings of the programme when it comes to their locality. Applications received by telephone and e-mail are then selected with the broadest possible representation in mind. Programme editor Nick Pisani puts it this way:

> We try and make sure that the balance between men and women is as good as it can be. We try to make sure that the age range is good, and that there is a full range of political opinion. We try to make sure that all ethnic groups within the community are properly represented in the audience.

Allowance is made in this process for the specific political characteristics of the locality where that week's programme is being recorded. 'If you are in Wolverhampton', says a producer, 'you want an audience that reflects the mood of Wolverhampton'.

To ensure a balance of party representation, local Conservative, Labour and Liberal parties (and the nationalist parties in Scotland and Wales) are invited to put a number of their supporters forward as potential audience members (*Any Questions?* uses the same technique). In the main, however, *Question Time's* public participants are self-selecting citizens – 'people who want to engage', in the view of presenter Dimbleby sifted to ensure balance by the production team. There is, of course, an obvious sense in which these volunteers are not representative of the average UK citizen so much as the ideal active citizen. That is an inevitable limitation on the representativeness of access which nothing in the programme makers' armoury can entirely overcome. Producers hope, however, that the consumption of access programmes by audiences at home will promote and encourage the kind of active citizenship being displayed by studio participants.

Both *Any Questions?* and *Question Time* are products of the public service BBC, which has a legal requirement to make a substantial amount of political broadcasting of quality. The UK's commercial channels operate under similar public service constraints, moderated by the need to attract sufficient advertising revenue to allow them pay to their way. For this reason, there is pressure on ITV, Channel 4 and Channel 5 to make programmes which are both political and popular. Responding to this mix of demands the commercial channels have over the years commissioned a number of innovative programme strands which have played an important role in extending access beyond the relatively narrow segments of the public served by *Any Questions?*

As of this writing, the flagship political access show on commercial television was Jonathan Dimbleby's eponymous programme for ITV, launched in 1995 and broadcasting in 2001 to an audience of between one and 1.5 million at Sunday lunchtime. *Jonathan Dimbleby*, like *Question Time*, aspires to what its presenter describes as 'a broad range in social class and all the other demographic terms'. Programme researchers aim for around 130 studio participants for each debate, selected and screened with a view to constructing a representative audience, politically and demographically. However, because the programme typically takes on one big topic per week (education, for example, or health), as opposed to a series of questions on topical issues, researchers aim for an audience which is not only representative, but personally involved to some extent with the issues raised in that week's discussion. An edition of the show devoted to the foot and mouth epidemic which affected British agriculture in early 2001 targeted farmers and others with a special interest in the issues. Some participants respond to on-air invitations, while others of a particular type required by the producers – young people, for example, who are generally less likely to volunteer for political access programmes – may be specifically targeted by contacting schools and universities.

Another ITV-sponsored innovation was the monarchy debate (*The Nation Decides*) produced by Carlton and broadcast over three hours in January 1997. This major experiment in public participation programming was introduced to viewers as 'the biggest live debate ever in the history of television, on the most contentious issue of the decade', a reference to the future of the British monarchy, even then (before the death of Princess Diana a few months later in August 1997) the subject of intense public and constitutional debate. The production brought together 3,000 people, divided into pro- and anti-monarchy camps, arranging them for dramatic effect in a circular arena surrounding a panel of pro- and anti-monarchy experts. Andrew Morton, the author of a ground-breaking biography of Diana Spencer, was included, as were an assortment of constitutional historians and journalistic commentators with strong opinions on the subject of the monarchy, such as novelist Frederick Forsyth and columnist Claire Rayner.

We have discussed the form and content of the monarchy debate in some detail elsewhere.[8] Its assembly of such a large group of the British people, in a uniquely irreverent discussion of an institution whose earthly representatives, as Andrew Morton pointed out during the debate, were but a few decades ago believed by one third of the public to be 'descended from God', lies at one extreme of a continuum of access programming styles bounded at the other by *Any Questions?* The latter's relatively passive style of public participation was here replaced by a passionate, at times rowdy crowd, encouraged in their passion and rowdiness by the gladiatorial style of the debate, the blunt tone of some of the panelists, and the inexperience of the chairman (TV presenter Roger Cook, better known before then as a presenter of door-stepping consumer programmes). The result was a noisy if compelling display of public participation in a debate of undoubted importance to the future of British democracy.

Members of the royal family were not present for these exchanges, of course – and all but the most rabid republican will have had some sympathy for what it must be like to have one's existence and *raison d'être* come under such attack in a public forum of this kind – but this was political access of a qualitatively new kind, in which the British public (3,000 in the arena, and millions more who participated in a telephone poll) received an unprecedented opportunity to express their feelings about the monarchy to which they are constitutionally subject.

For some critics, however, this was the moment when British public participation programming became too democratic. Conservative constitutional historian David Starkey, for example, speaking to a news journalist in the aftermath of the debate, suggested that it 'put a question mark over the future of the studio audience'. What the programme *actually* did was to reveal the kinds of hard questions many members of the British public had at this time about the future of the monarchy. In this sense the programme represented the British people to themselves, in a new kind of relationship to the monarchy, and not everybody liked what they saw and heard.

In this respect the monarchy debate highlighted the tensions inherent to any genuinely democratic polity, and the sometimes disruptive role which public participation media have the potential to play in it. Elsewhere we have referred to 'the crisis of mass representation'(McNair, 2000), meaning the collective anxiety provoked amongst some intellectuals when it is perceived that the people have gained too much access to the media, and are using that access to participate in political debates once monopolised by appropriately well-educated, 'rational' people like themselves. Public participation that is genuinely representative of the whole people (as opposed to its most educated and affluent sections only) *will* depart on occasion from the orderly debating conventions of parliament or the Oxbridge union, and may even degenerate at times into mediated mob rule, populist as well as popular; as tabloid as *Any Questions?* is broadsheet in tone. That does not necessarily make it any less democratic, however. On the contrary, truly democratic public participation *requires* the involvement of the masses in political debate, even when what they say makes for uncomfortable listening.

This ethos inspires the producers of *The Wright Stuff*, a day-time talk show broadcast by the UK's newest commercial TV network, Channel 5. The programme combines journalists and expert panelists with studio participants drawn from the public, complemented by thousands of phone callers and e-mailers who vote on the issues discussed. *The Wright Stuff* is included here not just because it was the only political access programme produced at the time of writing by the relatively impoverished Channel 5,[9] but because it deliberately sets out to extend mediated political debate to sections of the population hitherto excluded from it. The audience for *The Wright Stuff*, as for most day-time talk shows, is predominantly female (around 65 per cent of the programme's 180,000 viewers are women), and many of the topics discussed are of the human interest type featured on Oprah, Tricia and Kilroy, focused on the 'feminine' private sphere. Others are political in the sense defined above, addressing 'typically male' issues such as taxation.

This increasingly blurred distinction between the feminine private and the male public spheres – correctly identified by feminist analysts as a major and lingering limitation of political culture in a patriarchal society – is one which *The Wright Stuff*'s producers set out to challenge with an agenda which they proudly identify as 'tabloid': in presenter Jezz Wright's words, 'populist but not trashy, informed but not too worthy'. The broadcasters, he argues, 'have to get away from the notion that politics is only the domain of *Newsnight*,[10] etc.' *The Wright Stuff* seeks to make it also the domain of the day-time talk show audience – predominantly women, pensioners, and those out of work for various reasons. As editor Jezz Wright describes the programme concept: 'If it matters to you at home and if it is making the headlines you [the audience] get a chance to debate it and talk about it right there and then'.

Similarly 'tabloid' in their style and content are many of the radio phone-in programmes, such as the *Nicky Campbell* show, broadcast by BBC's Radio Five Live on weekday mornings between nine and twelve. This programme takes pride in extending opportunities for access to as broad a range of the British public as possible, widening the range of contributors beyond what the producer describes as the 'metropolitan chattering classes'. The editor of *Nicky Campbell* notes that:

> A lot of traditional journalists despise the phone-in format. They don't like what they consider to be uneducated views from people who aren't experts. Well, what we found is that there are a lot of experts out there, and if you've been working for twenty-five years in the health service I consider you to be an expert.

Another member of the *Nicky Campbell* production team observes that 'one of the guidelines we always use [for selecting topics] on the programme is – it needs to be the kind of thing that people are talking about in the pub'.

Though far from the deliberately provocative style of the US shock-jock, presenter Campbell has an assertive media presence and takes a more active role in steering the direction of the debate than the scrupulously neutral Dimbleby brothers on *Any Questions?* and *Question Time*. This reflects the qualities of the radio medium, as well as the programme's brief to involve and engage a broad mass audience. Given the lack of a visual dimension, the radio phone-in format is more dependent for its success on a distinctive, outspoken presenter who, while still required to work within the BBC's broad rules of impartiality and objectivity, has greater freedom to express a view on the issues under debate, or at least to articulate a no-nonsense version of what 'the people' think.

## Limits on representation

If the producers' efforts to broaden the reach of access programming – to make them part of a genuinely popular political culture – are consistent with the normative democratic principles set out earlier, their efforts to be as representative of the British people as possible are constrained by the simple fact that readiness to participate is not evenly distributed amongst that population. To the extent that participation in mediated politics, like other forms of civic engagement, is linked to the possession of what Putnam calls 'social capital', it is not surprising that those who respond to producers' invitations tend to be, as programme-makers themselves characterise it, male, middle-class, middle-aged and white.

In relation to social class, *Jonathan Dimbleby's* executive producer suggests that participants from less-educated, less-affluent social groups are more difficult to recruit because they do not frequent the types of community groups often targeted by researchers when assembling audiences for programmes, and they rarely apply for tickets independently.

On several of the mainstream access strands the preponderance of men over women amongst those applying to participate is pronounced. The producer of *Question Time* explains that 'It's sad to say it, but true that many more men than women apply to take part'. Producers on *Jonathan Dimbleby* observe that even when the studio audience is gender-balanced (because programme researchers intervene to make it so), men are more likely to make a contribution to the debate, particularly at the start of the programme. Women appear to be more reticent in these contexts, for reasons which are not entirely clear; a cultural hangover of patriarchy, perhaps, and the dominant role traditionally allotted men in the conduct of public discourse.

Radio phone-in programmes experience a similar problem. The rise of these programmes has coincided with the growth of the mobile telephone market. This technology enables participation by people outside their homes and on the move – most of whom, it appears from the observations of programme-makers, are men driving from one business meeting to another, or sitting in traffic jams on the M25 around London. The ratio of male to female callers to this programme is 70:30. Fifty five per cent of callers are men on mobile phones, aged 45-55. "Our average caller", says the producer, 'is a bloke in his late 40s, probably a driver, salesman, something like that, probably out on the road'.[11] A producer on the *Lesley Riddoch* show notes that 'it's definitely more males that ring the programme', while another expresses 'amazement' at the predominance of male callers.

To address gender and other kinds of imbalance, forms of positive discrimination are employed (as between particular age or ethnic groups, for example: one BBC producer notes 'We like to represent as many communities as possible, so that means, in simple terms, if you're black you're going to get on. If you're Asian you're going to get on'). The programme makers employ computer software packages which record the demographic profile of calls as they come in, and rank them according to what kind of caller is going to be required by that particular edition of the show. In a debate about feminism conducted on the *Nicky Campbell* show, for example, producers took care to ensure that women callers, though in a minority of all those who phoned-in, were not under-represented on air. Women callers are generally awarded thirty five 'points', where men get ten, promoting the former to the top of the producer's 'call-back' list (the list of those who, having expressed a desire to participate in debate, will be called back at some point during the programme and invited to contribute on air). Producers seek to ensure that female experts are regularly included in studio panels, on the basis that 'if you don't have any women guests on a phone-in, you won't get any female calls.' The presenter of the *Lesley Riddoch* show practises a form of positive discrimination by occasionally interrupting the flow of debate with appeals to female listeners to phone in and participate.

In these and other ways representation is actively worked for. Producers may also enlist the help of special interest groups with contacts in under-represented sectors of the public – youth organisations for young people; community groups for ethnic minorites, and so on. Programmes have been made especially for sections of the community identified as under-represented in the more mainstream strands like *Question Time*. Channel 4 has produced debates, usually late at night, specifically on ethnic minority issues, with those communities deliberately over-represented in the studio audience. *Trial by Night*, produced by Scottish television in the mid-1990s, is described by one of its presenters as being 'for a youth, student-type audience' of the type traditionally under-represented in public participation programming.

## Repeat performers

The representativeness of access programming may also be distorted by the over-participation of regulars, or 'repeat performers', as we have previously termed those who repeatedly appear in human interest access programmes (Hibberd et al, 2000). The people who volunteer to participate in political access programming do so for a variety of motives. Some are hobbyists who 'collect' appearances on political debate shows in the same way that some people are mildly addicted to appearing on human interest day-time talk shows. One participant on *Jonathan Dimbleby* confessed to us that 'I've been going to them [political access programmes] for about seven years', encouraged by the fact that 'once you get on the list they [programme researchers] ring you up all the time.' Says one participant on *The Wright Stuff*, who had previously been involved in eight or nine access programmes, 'I am interested in current affairs, and I do like to be on telly and have a say occasionally.'

Others are motivated by curiosity. 'I wanted to know how much of the programme was rigged,' says one *Question Time* participant, 'how much of it was set up and how much was organised'. A less sceptical participant stated: 'I admire the way David

Dimbeby chairs it, and I thought as it was local I would express an interest and come along to see what it was like ... It's understanding how a programme like this is made.'

> I was interested to be in an environment that I hadn't been in before, and see how they did all of that.

This last quote comes from a *Question Time* participant who was also, at the time of our interview, a Labour Party member. It is clear that many participants in access programming are more than averagely engaged in political affairs. They are more motivated to participate in political debate. Their political opinions are more worked out, and they are more confident in articulating those opinions. As a result, they are attractive to programme researchers. One interviewee who participated in an edition of *Jonathan Dimbleby* concerned with the issue of European union had been a member of the UK Independence Party (an organisation with strong views on Europe), and was now firmly established on the lists maintained by audience researchers on both *Question Time* and *Jonathan Dimbleby* (she was at the time of our research a Conservative Party member). She believes that 'they ring me up because I don't look bad on television', and because 'they've got to have somebody ... They often ring me up at short notice and say 'would you like to come on?' This source believes she is viewed by programme makers as a reliably voluble studio participant, especially on the issue of Europe. 'I can always ask a question if I want to.'

One producer interviewed for this study began his involvement with access programming as a regular of this kind, and admits at times to making up to eight phone calls, and appearing on three phone-in programmes per week. He had also appeared on more than one television access programme (*Question Time* and *Trial by Night*).

If they have good debating skills, then, and 'I know they are not mad', as one producer straightforwardly puts it, regulars may be welcomed as an aid to filling studio seats. They will often be included on the producer's data-base as individuals who can be relied upon to have a view, and actively sought out. In this respect, the aspiration to be representative does not override the production requirements of good TV or radio, nor does it mean allowing a random group of self-selecting participants to represent the public. Screening of applicants is common, both to ensure a balanced audience (in gender, class or ethnic terms), and a reliable supply of articulate participants.

Some repeat performers are less welcome. Programme makers on phone-in shows keep lists of problem individuals who call in habitually, and whose contributions are not required. At the time of our research the *Nicky Campbell* show had 984 such 'regulars' on its lists. Only one third of callers, indeed, were first-timers of the type preferred by phone-in programme makers. Those regulars regarded from previous experience as a nuisance are screened out by the same software packages which enable producers to improve the demographic balance on their programmes, and placed with other undesirables on a file of banned individuals, known to be unpredictable, potentially rule-breaking participants. On a live-to-air show such as *Jonathan Dimbleby*, screening out these individuals is essential. The producer of a leading access programme argues that:

> the viewer at home is not a political anorak. They want to see audience participation where people are asking the basic, straightforward questions that they want to ask themselves, and in which what is being articulated are the deeply felt fundamental aspirations of people. In other words, the worst audience contributor is a political anorak.

Representation can be skewed, finally, by the efforts of parties and lobbyists to pack audiences with their supporters – not 'anoraks', necessarily, but individuals whose aim is to give the media audience a particular, politically-motivated impression of how the public is thinking. During the London mayoralty election of 2000, one of the campaigns circulated an e-mail instructing supporters to try to get into the studio for a *Question Time* election special involving the main candidates. The producers became aware of this, and the attempt was thwarted. The example shows, however, that access programmes are perceived by increasingly media-focused political activists as 'pressure points' – as a *Question Time* producer describes it – to be targeted in the effort to get media publicity for a campaign. Some groups are better than others at exploiting the opportunities provided by access programmes for exposure. "The Countryside Alliance is very good", says one programme maker. 'The pro- and anti-abortionists are very good. Then there are organisations like the UK Men's Movement and Families Need Fathers. They're not very good. They're very easy to track, probably because they don't have many members.'

One limit on representation survives in UK access broadcasting as a matter of policy. We noted above that the US-style shock jock is not found in Britain outside a few of the more marginal and localised commercial radio stations. The public service broadcasting ethos of impartiality and balance continues to hold sway over both the BBC and the major commercial networks, tending to exclude aggressively opinionated, deliberately provocative presenters, especially in the sensitive area of political coverage. Participants, on the other hand, can be as opinionated and passionate as they like – are indeed frequently encouraged to be so – but cannot be allowed to express racist, misogynistic, homophobic or otherwise offensive views on air. All access programmes broadcast by the BBC are regulated by the organisation's Charter, which forbids such expressions, and requires programme-makers to devise ways of screening them out. *Question Time* is broadcast one hour after recording, partly to allow editing of contributions which breach the rules in this respect. Other programmes are transmitted with a brief time lag of a few minutes. Phone-in shows like *Nicky Campbell* and *Lesley Riddoch* seek to identify and exclude nuisance callers, and have been largely successful in doing so.

## Devolving access

An unavoidable form of skewing in access broadcasting – and thus a limit on the extent of programmes' representativeness - is the bias towards the participation of London audiences, and metropolitan audiences in general. The reasons for this bias are largely pragmatic. The main UK broadcasters are located in London and, for straightforward economic reasons, are inclined to produce most of their programmes there (although recent series of these programmes have involved noticeably more broadcasts outside of the London and South East). This inevitably means that Londoners tend to dominate the pool from which audiences for programmes like *Jonathan Dimbleby* and *Question Time* are drawn. The availability of this pool (twelve million people live in the greater London area) is an asset which, incidentally, assists broadcasters to more easily find participants drawn from ethnic and other minority groups (who are present there in larger numbers).[12]

However, a new challenge to metro-centrism in public participation broadcasting has arisen with the introduction of devolution to the UK by the Labour government of Tony Blair. There have long been political access programmes for the regions, of course, and for the nation-regions of Scotland, Wales and Northern Ireland, both on TV and radio. But devolution has made the construction of public access by UK-wide programmes more problematic, because more sensitive in an environment of heightened Scottish and Welsh national self-consciousness and politico-cultural distinctiveness. On the one hand, *Any Questions?* and *Question Time* have a remit to move around the UK, reflecting local issues and perspectives as they do so. On the other, they must maintain their appeal to a UK audience. Always a production challenge, getting the balance right has involved more delicate calculations as the assemblies in Wales and Northern Ireland, and the parliament in Scotland, take more of the functions of government from Westminster, and as the distinctive political party balances of these parts of the UK sharpen further. If the subject of these programmes is politics, then producers have to decide whose politics they are talking about – those of Westminster, Edinburgh, Cardiff or Belfast? They must also ask – can these distinctive politics be made relevant to TV and radio audiences in London or Liverpool?

Our view is that they can, and they should be. Britain's status as a multi-nation state is hardly new, after all, and the country has always harboured strong local and regional identities within and between the nations which comprise it. Devolution for Scotland, Wales and Northern Ireland recognises the UK's diversity, and related developments like the introduction of elected mayoralties (with regional assemblies for England on the political agenda) will give it enhanced constitutional recognition. As devolution proceeds at various levels thoughout the UK (and assuming that one wishes to see the preservation of the UK as a political entity) the availability of mass mediated public debates covering both local and UK-wide issues could take on a heightened role in maintaining a British (as opposed to a Scottish, Welsh or Northern Irish) public sphere. In January 2003, for example, to launch a new run of the strand, the producers of *Question Time* broadcast from Belfast. This was a time when the Northern Ireland assembly was in suspension, and the political situation in the province was tense. The expert panel included members of the SDLP, Sinn Fein, the Democratic Unionist Party and the Official Unionists. Although panellists and studio participants discussed UK-wide issues such as the prospect of war in Iraq, much of the programme was concerned with the complexities of the sectarian politics which dominate Northern Ireland. Arcane and despair-inducing as these debates often seem to an audience outside Northern Ireland itself, they are of crucial importance to the British Isles, and require to be aired. *Any Questions?* and *Question Time*, by combining local and UK-wide issues in this way, represent the British national to the local and vice versa. They are, indeed, the only UK-wide journalistic media which routinely do so (apart from circumstances in which local news stories acquire UK-wide newsworthiness). Given the crucial role of broadcasting in this respect, how do access programme makers currently address the devolution challenge?

## Devolved access – the Scottish case

In 1999, Scotland became a devolved nation within the United Kingdom. The new powers acquired under the Scotland Act 1999 in many ways reinforced the fact of Scottish distinctiveness. The nation acquired its own Parliament and Executive and very rapidly Scotland's press and broadcasting focused news attention on the new political institutions (Schlesinger et al, 2001). Scotland has long had an influential indigenous press, which continues to exercise a strong grip on the country's readership, despite recent inroads made by London-based titles. In the field of public service radio and television broadcasting, the country is served by BBC Scotland, with headquarters in Glasgow. Alongside this, also regulated on public service lines, are the ITV companies Scottish Television and Grampian Television. Between them they cover virtually the whole country and are owned by the Scottish Media Group (SMG). The dominant commercial radio player is Scottish Radio Holdings. A small slice of the television audience is served by Border Television. The BBC, Channel 3 (ITV), Channel 4 and Channel 5 all have obligations to spend varying proportions of their programme-making budgets outside of London on first-run productions. Part of this expenditure occurs in Scotland and is crucial to sustaining the creative economy there, as in other parts of the UK. Both the BBC and Channel 4 commission programmes for the network (as well as for Scotland) through their nations and regions offices in Glasgow.

Curiously, devolution has had a paradoxical outcome in terms of the amount of access programming that is aired north of the border. During the 1990s – in the pre-devolutionary years – a number of broadcasts, in different ways, sought to bring the audience into the arena of political and public debate. Scottish Television broadcast programmes such as *Scottish Voices*, *The Scottish 500* (notably during election periods) and *Trial by Night*. The last of these sought to be especially accessible to young people, with a formula that was 'a cross between a chat show and a current affairs debate', in the words of one of its presenters, Charlene Sweeney. Another long-running stalwart of the mid-1990s schedules was Scottish Television's *Scottish Women*, which addressed a mix of topical and human interest issues, using a presenter in interaction with a studio audience of women. Scottish adapted the format of the monarchy debate for its public particiaption special on the devolution referendum, broadcast in September 1997. For its part, BBC Scotland broadcast *Words with Wark*, which addressed newsworthy political topics before a studio audience and an expert panel of professional politicians, with debate steered by the presenter. The programme, which went off the air in 1999, was fronted by Kirsty Wark, well known to network viewers as a regular presenter of *Newsnight* on BBC 2.

When we began our research during 2000, the year after devolution had arrived in Scotland, we found that audience access programming had largely disappeared from the television schedules north of the border. The BBC and the SMG-owned commercial companies, Scottish TV and Grampian TV, all responded to the new political dispensation by developing a variety of specialist political programmes on television. These – *Newsnight Scotland*, *Holyrood* (now restyled as *Scottish Politics*), *Holyrood Live*, *Crossfire* – all centred on the doings of the political class and on current policy issues, but contained no element of public participation. Scottish Television's *Platform* came on air not long before this book went to press, and mixes interview and expert analysis with live debate. Otherwise, though, since 1999 Scottish audiences have been more reliant than before on networked current affairs programmes to offer them access to political debate.

There are inherent limits to how UK-wide access programming can match onto the current Scottish political communications map. Despite clear evidence of good intent (London-based programme teams make adjustments to established formulae to meet Scottish needs), they must keep the entire UK audience in mind.

The fact that Scotland has a distinctive political map and electoral cycle throws up further complications. Even before devolution, Scotland's distinctive political culture would create the occasional difficulty for London schedulers. A well-known case occurred when the networked programme *Panorama* intended to run an interview with the Conservative Prime Minister John Major in the spring of 1995, three days before the Scottish local elections. A legal move by opposition parties in Scotland succeeded in preventing the broadcast by way of an interdict from the High Court in Edinburgh on the grounds that it breached the impartiality rule (Barendt, 1998: p. 111).

There can be no doubt that, after devolution, network broadcasters have to be even more sensitive to local politics. When the ITV network broadcast *Ask the Prime Minister* in the winter of 2000, it once again faced protests about impartiality. The network had scheduled a programme with Prime Minister Tony Blair and an audience of questioners. The programme was due to be screened before a routine parliamentary by-election in Falkirk West. It was, however, also a time when speculation was rife about whether there would be a UK general election the following spring. Transmitting an access programme of this kind featuring Mr Blair was a technical breach of the Representation of the People Act. In order to ensure due impartiality, ITV had to reschedule its programmes in

Scotland. It also added a special edition of the election programme, *Hustings*, to meet the objections of the SNP.[13]

Looked at from London, therefore, Scotland presents a practical problem for network programmes, although by no means an insuperable one. We asked the production staff on BBC1's *Question Time* how they viewed their task post-devolution. The programme's editor, Nick Pisani, conceived of his programme as 'a sort of national institution', with 'national' here equating to the UK as a whole. *Question Time* was created before the televising of Parliament and has survived into a new era – one in which (unlike Westminster) the devolved legislatures of Scotland, Wales and Northern Ireland have all eagerly embraced the television age in an effort to make themselves more accessible. One of the more recent innovations undertaken by *Question Time* (see chapter four) is to have two non-party panelists (often including celebrities or entertainers) in order to broaden the programme's audience appeal. However, devolution has cut across this audience-building tactic, as Pisani noted:

> Devolution obviously poses a problem for a programme like *Question Time* which is broadcast throughout the United Kingdom, because you have to make a programme that is appealing to people throughout the UK. There are four [major] parties here [in Scotland][14] which means that you can't really have your two non-political panelists. The dynamic is different, but the challenge is to make a programme as relevant to the audience here in the studio, relevant to the audience here in Scotland, but not alienating to the audience in London or Brighton or Cardiff or Wolverhampton. So there is no point in us coming to Scotland and just discussing detailed Scottish political matters for an hour because not many people outside Scotland will be very interested in that and there are plenty of programmes in Scotland where that can take place.

Pisani is clear about the legitimate limitations of network broadcasting's capacity to engage with Scottish issues. *Question Time* has to address two overlapping communicative communities when it is in Scotland (as it must also do in Wales or Northern Ireland). Not surprisingly, David Dimbleby, the programme's veteran presenter, shares Pisani's perspective. He adds:

> What we do is usually take one out of the five questions on a local issue – that's to say a national Scottish issue or national Welsh issue or national Northern Irish issue – and then try to make the other questions about [things] that apply to the whole of the UK. … But … four out of your five panellists are local politicians on the whole and that does make for a very difficult problem, because they'll all be concentrating on their patch and trying to bring things back to what's happening in Scotland or what's happening in Wales.

In this way, the recognition of constitutional change and its consequences is limited by everyday questions of programme practice and aesthetics: how to go about the selection of an appropriate panel and of suitable questions (from the point of view of the democratic political process), while making watchable (or listenable) programmes for the wider UK audience. One of the *Any Questions?* production team explained that in editions of the programme recorded in Scotland especially careful consideration had to be given to the composition of the programme's panel. *Any Questions?* has only four panel members and in the devolved nations – unlike in England – account has to be taken both of coalition politics and the existence of nationalist parties. *Any Questions?* – just like *Question Time* – also pays close attention to the mix of questions that is selected from the studio audience. As one of the production staff remarked:

> If you get four Scots together they want to talk about nothing but Scotland whereas we are a national programme. Now they would say, 'Oh well, you're a national programme and we have to listen to – 99 per cent of the time – English issues ... [Now] I have this policy: I have two English, two Scots, and I think out of the seven questions we're likely to do a couple Scottish, the rest English. ... I think the idea of having just four Scots doing seven Scottish questions ... is a disaster. It just makes it less and less relevant, less and less interesting and more and more ghettoised. ... I try to disperse more Scots on English panels and if they're good it makes no difference, they just happen to be Scottish, don't they? It's not a big deal: they are not the token Scot, [but rather] a good performer who happens to be Scottish.

Jonathan Dimbleby, chairman of *Any Questions?*, and presenter of *ITV's Jonathan Dimbleby* was sensitive to the fact that 'it may seem from Scotland [that] you're watching a foreign country's issues'. However, if the content were too Scottish he believes that in England 'fifty million plus people are going to say, "Why are we watching this?"' Dimbleby acknowledges that English audiences need to be kept abreast of developments in Wales and Scotland, 'but I sometimes wonder, is it like reporting back from Ethiopia? 'This is happening here and you show know about it''. The comparison made with distant foreign reporting underlines the view of some observers that devolution has increased internal differences inside the UK. At the time of our study, Dimbleby believed that the problems of working across the different public domains had still not been fully resolved by access programme-makers.

In radio, BBC Scotland has boosted its conventional political analysis with programmes such as *Politics Tonight*. It has also explicitly responded to devolution by creating *Lesley Riddoch*, a weekday programme that runs from 12.05 to 2.00 p.m., fronted by one of Scotland's best-known women journalists. As of this writing, this was the sole regular political access slot in post-devolution Scottish broadcasting.

A number of features are designed to make it as appealing as possible. The presenter, Lesley Riddoch, is noted for a highly direct style of engaging with her audience and for being both a persistent questioner and one who is prepared to cut people off if they stray from the point. As Sharon Mair, the programme's senior producer has commented:

> We have a very strong presenter and she's very identified with the programme. Her commitment to the programme is really strong and she defines the tone of the programme. She has really good journalistic credentials as well.

The programme team tries to find strong stories that generate debate each day. It also aims to find those who are directly involved in such stories and to have them contribute to debate, thus departing from a strictly party-political driven agenda. There is a policy of taking debate out of the studio to a range of locations in Scotland in order to build a relationship with local audiences. As Mair puts it:

> We need to have a bit of colour and texture. We quite often go out on the streets and get reaction, on the phone, on the street, or from the satellite van on the street and still have Lesley in the studio. Also one of the remits of the programme is to be out and about.

Producers see it as part of their mission to travel around Scotland, both to build the audience and to ensure contact with the regional diversity of the country. At the time of our research, the team had been to the Highlands, the Borders and a range of Scottish towns and cities. As one of the programme's researchers put it: 'I think one of the most important things we actually do is outside broadcasts and taking the programme to various parts of Scotland because it often lets people know that there is a programme.' He went on to observe that because the programme was on Radio Scotland and was a 'national platform' it had to cover the whole of the country. The programme team also saw themselves as needing to encourage people to speak up who might sometimes be reluctant to give voice to their opinions especially during outside broadcasts, though they had sometimes found very articulate contributors on location.

The programme is conceived as 'the national radio phone-in', with a particular interest in the 35-55 age range. Here 'the nation' is defined as Scottish rather than British. Like other programmes of this kind, *Lesley Riddoch* is interactive, with e-mail traffic coming in alongside telephone calls. The callers and e-mailers sometimes become studio guests and contributors. The fact that it is broadcast over the web also means that it attracts reactions from the far-flung Scottish diaspora. The programme team told us of e-mails coming from the USA and New Zealand, for instance.

There is no pan-Scottish station in commercial radio north of the border. However, Scot-FM did broadcast a series of six monthly political access debates in the run-up to the June 2001 general election. The series was called *The Scottish Six* and transmitted between 6.00 and 7.00 p.m. Sponsorship came from prominent bodies in Scottish civil society such as the local authorities' convention (CoSLA), the Scottish TUC and the Law Society of Scotland. The station had an unusually large speech target under its licence – 51 per cent – and running such a series was seen as a good audience-building strategy, according to its then head of news, current affairs and sport, Glenn Campbell. The programmes were located in the smaller towns of the central belt – the station's target area – as part of a policy of developing a local sense of ownership of the station.[15]

## The Communications Bill and the future of access programmes in Scotland

As we have seen, access programmes in Scotland are distinctly thin on the ground, with the sole exception of BBC Radio where *Lesley Riddoch* is a centrepiece of the daytime schedule. The future of access programmes on television and on radio will now depend on the new media order being ushered in by the forthcoming Communications Act. How the Act will be implemented and regulated by Ofcom, the Office of Communications, will affect Scotland's media economy, like that of the other nations and regions of the UK, and that in turn will determine the scope and range of programming. At the time of writing, as the Bill has completed its second reading, the broad lines of policy concerning the nations and regions are fairly clear, although the Communications Bill still had to complete its passage through Parliament at Westminster.[16]

A striking feature of UK communications legislation is the retention of regulatory powers in London post-devolution. The state's powers over broadcasting and telecommunications – which are the centrepiece of the Communications Act – are 'reserved' by the Westminster parliament. The political logic of decentralisation, however, and the predominantly technological and economic logic of media concentration, on the other, pull in opposite directions. This may throw up tensions over time and how these are managed will be a major test of skill and resolve for Ofcom.

There are both political and economic calculations behind the refusal to devolve powers over the media. Politically, and most notably in relation to broadcasting, there has been a fear in political circles and among senior broadcasters that parcelling out powers will lead inevitably to the collapse of the Union. Lord (John) Birt, a former Director-General of the BBC, reflected in his memoirs on his opposition to BBC Scotland broadcasting its own international, national and local news at 6.00 p.m. on BBC 1, the so-called 'Scottish Six'. The debate about this became a *cause célèbre* in Scotland, with distant echoes in London.

> I was deeply resistant to the proposal. It could have dire consequences for the BBC and unintended consequences for the United Kingdom. ... The end of a single common experience of UK news would encourage separatist tendencies (Birt, 2002, p.484).

Many would find Birt's apocalytic view of the implications of changing the scheduling of one network news bulletin to be far-fetched. But the underlying attitude he expressed about the stakes involved in retaining UK-level control clearly does inform the Communications Bill. We may assume that for the foreseeable future, communications generally, and broadcasting in particular, will remain a key part of Westminster's remit. Arguments about the provision of programmes in the nations and regions, therefore, will take place within this political and regulatory framework.

Economically, the thinking underlying the Communications Act has been summed up in the oft-repeated mantra that introduced the legislation. Government policy is intended to make 'the UK the most dynamic and competitive communications market in the world'.[17] Increased competitiveness is conceived of as occurring within a 'convergent' digital electronic environment. For British policy-makers, the key reference point is the global economy and building 'UK plc's' strengths within that context. Permitting the emergence of bigger players – for instance, a single ITV – easing cross-media ownership rules, and encouraging foreign investment are all part of this picture.

The Communications Bill and Ofcom have not been born into a vacuum, however. A key legacy of the British broadcasting system, as it moves into its new phase, is the now long-standing commitment to sustaining regional identities and also to maintaining broadcast production outside the M25 belt surrounding London. While at one level there are intense pressures to face outwards and address the global market, there are also constraints that mean that audiences in the nations and regions have to be served in ways continuous with the past. We do know that there is a considerable appetite for news provision that addresses local and regional concerns (Hargreaves and Thomas, 2002). We also know that regional programming more generally is regarded as a vital service by the vast majority of viewers (Kidd and Taylor, 2002). Arguably, the growing devolutionary consciousness in various parts of England may reinforce this. The need to assure the continuing supply of regional programming in television has been recognised in the legislation and by the regulator, not least in order to sustain the broadcast economy outside London (ITC, 2002). It is reasonable to suppose, therefore, that the nations and regions will continue to be significant in the future communications environment. However, Ofcom may well have to be very robust to safeguard this part of its remit from centralising pressures. In Scotland, while distinctively Scottish news and current affairs reporting are certain to remain a feature of the new Scottish polity, on present post-devolutionary form there is little reason to suppose that there will be a new upsurge of access programming either on radio or television.

## Notes

1  Although we do not address their role in this study, readers' letters are clearly still of great importance in permitting the consumers of particular print media to communicate with each other about politics. They also act as a channel through which both broadsheet and tabloid newspapers strive to influence political elites with demonstrations of the force of their readers' opinions.

2  Reported by ITN's then editor-in-chief Richard Tait, at the Stirling symposium on access and broadcasting.

3  Following our research Scot FM was taken over by the Guardian Media Group's Real Radio.

4  In the 1990s Channel Four broadcast a series of People's Parliaments, an attempt to construct an "informed democracy" on television, as the head of news and current affairs at Channel Four puts it. In close association with James Fishkin, Professor of Government at the University of Austin, Texas, the People's Parliaments adopted a "deliberative model" in trying to "energise the democratic process on TV". The programme assembled three hundred people selected by an authoritative market research agency, polled them on their attitudes to a particular issue, exposed them to 48 hours of information and discussion of that issue, then polled them again to assess how their opinions had been altered by their exposure.

5   The show's producer took great pains to explain to the assembled audience, before the live broadcast began, that every effort had been made to find a suitably qualified female panelist, and she apologised for the failure to do so.

6   Here and subsequently, unless otherwise indicated, all quotes attributed to programme-makers were obtained by the research team in interviews conducted between October 2000 and May 2001.

7   One young focus group respondent, when asked about *Any Questions?*, observed: "I don't listen to Radio Four from any principle, but because my parents are teachers. It's like, "we are teachers, we must listen to Radio Four". So I've always had to... I always listen to Radio Four because I have been forced to listen to it by my parents". On the other hand, after the programme from which these comments are taken the producers of *Any Questions?* recorded an edition in Brixton College, and claim that they broadcast from more inner city institutions than any other access programme.

8   See McNair, 2000, pp.118-120.

9   The Wright Stuff was not the first political access programme on Channel 5, however. Between 1997 and 1999 the channel broadcast a Sunday evening debate show chaired by Kirsty Young which addressed, among other subjects, the legalisation of cannabis.

10  A late-night minority audience news and current affairs programme on BBC 2.

11  Producers note similar difficulties on programmes not included in this study, such as Late Night Live, a late night phone-in show broadcast to the London region.

12  On the other hand, says the editor of Jonathan Dimbleby, 'London audiences are much more used to telly and the media, so they're not as good at responding [to calls for participants]. It's not such a big deal for them"

13  Reflecting the seriousness with which party protests can be viewed, Steve Anderson, ITV's head of news and current affairs, observed: "Once the SNP made their point, you know, we replied to them. We took our measures to make sure Falkirk West was not going to be referred to in the programme. We never took any phone calls from the constituency. We never allowed anybody to talk about it. Tony Blair was told he couldn't talk about the Falkirk West by-election. So, you know, we did as much as we could to ensure that nobody could accuse us of influencing the vote".

14  Four major ones – the Labour Party and the Liberal Democrats, in coalition at the time of writing, and the Scottish National Party and the Conservatives, both in opposition. In the 1999-2003 Scottish Parliament, there was also Green Party and Scottish Socialist Party representation, and one independent. All increased their share of the vote in the 2003 election.

15  The question of connecting to local and regional views and experiences is important for the Scottish media, where localism and regionalism are asserted regularly, and are expressed in media consumption patterns. If one of the macro issues about broadcasting today consists of Scots feeling under-served by UK programmes that privilege English issues, as they see it, another frequently articulated complaint comes from those who often feel that too much attention is lavished on Edinburgh and Glasgow by the Scottish media. We detected this current in one of our focus groups in the Stirling area, where geographical resentments about the two big cities were also compounded by those of class, as it was believed that the articulate and educated were unduly favoured in those selected to pose questions in access programmes.

16  The Communications Bill was published 20 November 2002, after substantial revisions of the Draft Bill, and was passed as the Communications Act in Autumn 2003.

17  www.communicationsbill.gov.uk/policynarrative/550806.html

# 4

# Constructing Access, II: Interrogation and Mobilisation

Parallelling the process whereby public access broadcasting has become more representative over time, the exercise of critical scrutiny it aspires to provide – its *interrogative* function – has become more intense and aggressive.

As already noted, the *Any Questions?* model of critical scrutiny reflects the political culture of the 1940s which gave it birth. Members of the audience set the agenda, in so far as the questions asked of panelists are drawn from the many provided by the audience in advance. With rare exceptions, however, their role does not go beyond the asking of questions, and the provision of mild applause or boos in response to panelists' replies. Participants in *Any Questions?* are encouraged to be a polite, restrained audience, and appear in the main satisfied to put their questions and sit back while the experts on the stage before them address the issues raised. On occasion the chairman will invite a questioner to give his or her view of the panelists' comments, but the tone of such follow-ons rarely goes beyond polite disagreement.

This is not in itself intended as a criticism. The audience for *Any Questions?*, in the studio listening at home, understands and accepts the rules which govern the programme, and would probably be uncomfortable with the more raucous style of, say, the monarchy debate (see Chapter Three). There are also, argues chairman Jonathan Dimbleby when defending the distinctively restrained ambience of his studio set up, resource constraints on a programme produced by the cinderella medium of radio. These make it difficult to construct a flowing, audience-centred debate.

> It's more difficult in radio to maintain the pace of the programme if you have lots of microphones going around. You have to search for the person and there will be silences.

On a TV programme like *Question Time*, by contrast, there are visuals to compensate for these silences, as cameras pan around the hundred or so faces of the people assembled for debate and often eager to join in.

The interrogatory style of *Any Questions?*, like its reliance on a particular type of audience participant is the consequence of its origins in a very different kind of political culture from that of the early twenty first century. Elsewhere in the public sphere (including on programmes fronted by Dimbleby for other channels) realising the interrogatory function of public participation programming means enabling audiences to do more than sit passively before government ministers or party leaders as they talk or answer questions. In today's political environment access has to be more than merely symbolic: it must be accompanied by the visible, relatively unconstrained participation of citizens in robust debate with their governors. When it works, argues Jonathan Dimbleby, 'it really does serve as a substitute for the best kind of hustings'. As David Dimbleby put it to the *Question Time* studio audience in an effort to prepare them for a recording of the show observed by the authors in November 2000, this is 'your programme'. The audience on this occasion were instructed to approach their involvement in it 'like a robust Victorian town hall meeting', encouraged to express their dissatisfaction, anger or approval of the answers provided by panelists to their questions. Editor Nick Pisani declares of *Question Time* that 'it's the audience's show. They set the agenda, they choose the questions. They write the questions'. Not only that, they answer back if they feel their questions have not been adequately answered. Members of the audience who have not asked a question formally are also invited to intervene in debate. David Dimbleby explains that as chairman of *Question Time* he has tried:

> to strengthen the role of the audience in the asking of questions, and to encourage a feeling of debate between the audience and the people on the panel. All my efforts have been towards making the audience feel that it's their programme...the aim being to satisfy the audience at home that the pertinent questions of that week have been asked, and that the people taking part are being pushed a bit on those questions, not by me but by the audience, with me chivvying occasionally from the side.

Its success in pioneering a more active public participation in political debate since its 1979 launch has allowed *Question Time* to become what its producer calls 'a sort of national institution, born of a time before live cameras [were allowed] in parliament'. This was 'a different political time, when parliament was supreme, and relatively invisible, and your political masters were relatively inaccessible.' *Question Time* challenged that inaccessability, and was therefore something of a televisual event when it appeared. If its status as a national institution has been reduced by the more frequent appearance of senior politicians in a variety of media contexts, the programme has undoubtedly contributed much to the emergence of a political culture in which access to – and critical scrutiny by – the people, through the media, has come to be seen as a professional requirement of the working politician.[1] Dimbleby observes that 'the people who choose to come to *Question Time* are much more likely to want to argue a case or debate than they were five years ago'. For Pisani:

> Its attraction continues to be that ordinary members of the public can question and challenge and take on those who govern them, or form their opinions, or influence society in some way or other.

Over on ITV, studio audiences on the *Jonathan Dimbleby* show are part of what its presenter calls 'a shared process' of interrogation of politicians; a 'combination of audience participation with a very aggressive interview', as the programme editor describes the format. The programme typically begins with a face-to-face interview by Dimbleby of that week's political guest (usually a senior minister or opposition equivalent), lasting twenty minutes or more, after which members of the studio audience put questions and make comments of their own. The adversarial interview is a well-established tool of British political journalism, of course,[2] and Jonathan Dimbleby has long been one of its most effective practitioners. This particular interviewing slot, as chapter two described, is based on an earlier ITV programme presented by Brian Walden, renowned at the time for its tough, persistent style. Walden confronted his interviewees alone, however, without the involvement of members of the public. While the in-depth interview format has some clear advantages, such as allowing an experienced professional inquisitor the time to explore issues often in forensic detail, without regard to the needs of a studio audience, it can often become a battle of rhetorical wits between two gladiators, each pursuing his or her own insular agenda. In the view of the producers of *Jonathan Dimbleby* their combination of the aggressive, adversarial interview with critical questioning and comment from the public enhances the effectiveness of both techniques for subjecting political elites to critical scrutiny.

The fact that the interview takes place before an assembled studio audience makes it more difficult, in Jonathan Dimbleby's view, for the experienced interviewee to apply the usual evasive tactics. 'Politicians who are any good,' he judges, 'will be unnerved at the prospect of dissembling in a way that can be discerned by members of the audience,' because that same audience will shortly be wading into the debate. He can therefore, in his own opinion, extract more honesty and spontaneity in replies to his questions, as well as brief the audience and put them in a position to ask incisive and revealing questions. Having watched and listened to the interview, studio participants' questions are not rehearsed or scripted, but spontaneous. Says the editor, 'once they're in there, then if they put their hand up and Jonathan picks them, they could say literally anything.' The senior producer describes the programme's ethos in the following terms: 'Get an audience in and hold the politicians to account.'

In so far as these programmes frequently involve senior politicians they represent a highly distinctive feature of British political culture. In few comparable democracies are leading politicians expected to confront members of the public live on-air. Other countries have access programmes, of course. The USA, as noted in chapter one, has its legions of radio phone-in shows, but these tend not to involve senior politicians. CNN's *Larry King Live* invites viewers to phone-in or e-mail questions and comments but the programme's style, even on the rare occasions it involves senior politicians in topical debate, is far removed from the adversarial intensity of public participation broadcasting in the UK. Australia has the ABC-produced *Australia Talks*, which has provided TV viewers in that country with an access experience similar in form to that of *Question Time* in the UK.

Although a national broadcast, edition of this programme seen by the authors in autumn 2001 featured only minor politicians and local celebrities engaged in debating local issues. Also in Australia, Channel Seven's *Sixty Minutes* allows lively public debates on current issues, though conducted in the absence of an expert panel drawn from the political elite. *Meet the Press* puts senior politicians before an interrogatory audience of journalists, but the public are not involved.

In Australia, as in many countries, the scrutinising role of access is limited by the reluctance of senior politicians to participate. On *Question Time* and *Any Questions?*, by contrast, Cabinet ministers, party leaders and even prime ministers are regular guests. For the producer of *Question Time* the programme provides 'face to face contact with the people who govern you'. And for the majority of those in the studio audience, 'it's a once-in-a-lifetime opportunity to challenge a person in authority.'

To protect the perceived authenticity and integrity of this challenge broadcasters stress the spontaneity of the debates. On occasion they have been required to resist the efforts which politicians and their advisers make to influence, manipulate or bully them. The studio debate shows (*Any Questions?* and *Question Time*) routinely remind audiences that politicians on the panel have no advance knowledge of the questions they will be asked (although a well-briefed politician familiar with the format will have a good idea of what is likely to come up). We were told that when prime minister Tony Blair first appeared on the *Nicky Campbell* programme one of his media advisers insisted on sitting with the producer as calls came in. The producer resisted this demand, in the belief that it would dilute the spontaneity of the forthcoming debate, and eventually the adviser submitted to being excluded from the studio. On another occasion, to coincide with the delivery of an important speech, Blair's office offered the *Nicky Campbell* team an exclusive hour of live access to the prime minister. The programme makers, it was stressed, would be able to operate their standard procedures, deciding the agenda and selecting phone-in participants in the normal way, although the timing of the broadcast would be dictated by the timing of Blair's speech. Following their guidelines in such situations producers referred the proposal up to senior BBC management, who declined on the grounds that 'they [Blair's office] decided on the timing and therefore, to a certain extent, they would have set the agenda on that day.' In this case the risks of being perceived as susceptible to political manipulation outweighed the prestige which going ahead with the exclusive broadcast would have accorded the *Nicky Campbell* show, Radio Five Live, and the BBC in general.

## Access and elections

Nowhere is the 'substitute hustings' function of access programming more important than during election campaigns. The UK general election of 2001 confirmed that in an age when the tradition of public meetings and town hall hustings has largely gone, and when politicians are generally protected from spontaneous encounters with ordinary people, *mediated access*, facilitated through the electronic channels of TV, radio and increasingly the Internet, is the closest most people come to engaging with those who are competing for their votes in elections. The 2001 general election campaign confirmed that there is in British electoral politics today an expectation that political leaders will meet media audiences in adversarial, interrogatory contexts where they must answer to the people, or at least to a *sampled public* which is in some sense representative of the people. Pierre Bourdieu called French access TV a 'charade' in his pessimistic book-length essay *On Television and Journalism* (1998). In Britain, however, and especially during elections, access broadcasting has become a key moment in the critical scrutiny of politicians. Where the American campaign highlights the live presidential debate involving the major candidates in high-profile stand-offs (where agendas are subject to intense negotiation, and with questions put not by members of the public but by senior journalists), British political leaders have shied away from head-to-head confrontations outside the highly ritualised procedures of the House of Commons (where, of course, they regularly debate with each other in parliamentary debates). Unlike US presidential candidates, however, they do submit themselves to genuinely spontaneous encounters with small groups of people who have been selected to participate in access programmes.

They may not want to do so, of course, because the form removes much of the control over presentation which the modern politician is used to. David Dimbleby observes that:

> For most politicians *Question Time* is the biggest audience they appear before during the normal year, and it happens to be a rather robust forum because if 150 people think you're talking nonsense they let it show. It's quite alarming, I think.

Politicians, including the most senior, regularly appear on these programmes nonetheless, because in the contemporary political culture of the UK it is expected of them, and because their competitors are doing so. To refuse in these circumstances risks projecting a political message of inaccessability and aloofness which reflects badly on the aspiring politician.

Although the UK has a tradition of involvement by senior politicians in public participation programming from *Any Questions?* onwards, this has not until recently extended to the Prime Minister him or herself, for whom one of the privileges of executive office has been to be protected from the uncertainties and potential indignities of live public debate, especially on TV. Until Tony Blair's emergence, mediated access to the executive was limited to contexts in which the Prime Minister could expect the broadcasters to protect him or her from unscripted criticism or abuse. Margaret Thatcher, for example, who broke tradition by appearing while still Prime Minister on at least one entertainment-oriented television chat show, was interviewed several times on BBC Radio Two's *Jimmy Young Show*. But on only one occasion — an edition of the *Nationwide* programme broadcast by the BBC during the 1983 general election, shortly after the conclusion of the Falklands war in 1982 – did she allow herself to be confronted by a member of the public, who was critical of the prime minister's role. A Mrs Diane Gould challenged Thatcher on the legal and moral grounds for sinking the Argentine battleship Belgrano during the 1982 Falklands War. The tenacity of her questioning led to a heated exchange with Mrs Thatcher, leading many commentators to appreciate for the first time the role the public can play in tackling their elected representatives on important political issues. As Sylvia Harvey argues:

> The persistence of Mrs Gould's questioning and argument provoked (if only momentarily) a response of angry incoherence from the Prime Minister, producing a remarkable television spectacle and a recorded public encounter dangerous for the reputation of any politician (2000, p.160).

Thatcher's visible anger and impatience with her questioner damaged her reputation, and came to exemplify the dangers posed politicians by exposing themselves to the public in contexts where they have little or no control over the terms of the exchange. Neither Margaret Thatcher nor her successor John Major ever participated in a live studio debate with an audience of ordinary citizens, outside of a general election period, when John Major appeared on *Question Time*.

It was a significant moment, then, when in 2000 ITV broadcast the first of what its producers hoped would be a series of *Ask the Prime Minister* specials, made by the same company, and chaired by the same presenter, as are responsible for *Jonathan Dimbleby*. *Ask the Prime Minister* placed public participation at its centre, with the prime minister interrogated both by Dimbleby and an assembled studio audience. The exchange reached a peak-time ITV audience of 5.25 million, representing 25 per cent of the available audience for that time slot (regarded as 'respectable' by ITV's network head when interviewed for this study). Opinions will vary, of course, as to the degree of critical scrutiny of the prime minister which took place on the programme, but there can be little doubt that the debate *was* spontaneous and unscripted, and that Blair had to work hard to satisfy his interrogators.

For chairman Jonathan Dimbleby, the programme was 'high theatre. You weren't going to get a cool, detached analysis but you saw the Prime Minister under pressure, under fire. You were able to judge him by his performance, his demeanour. I think it did the political process good.' For the head of the ITV network, which commissioned *Ask the Prime Minister*, the interaction between Blair and the studio audience which it allowed demonstrated that 'the age of deference has gone. I've never seen the prime minister under such pressure, and there was no escape'. Nor did there seem to be any desire to escape on Blair's part. On the contrary, he submitted to very similar pressure when he appeared on a special edition of *Question Time* broadcast during the 2001 general election campaign (see below, pp.84-85). In a context where there were relatively few 'negatives' on which the media could seriously criticise New Labour, and amidst a campaign generally perceived as intensively managed by all parties, this was a rare moment of reality intrusion.

As the head of the ITV network put it, on the basis of these and other examples since 1997, access programmes have made an important contribution to making politicians more accountable.

> The political establishment has had its own way for far too long with broadcasting in this country. It's been able to set the terms all the time about the conditions on which it will go on programmes, what questions are going to be asked, how they're going to be treated. The viewers can see through all this crap now. They're not children. They're not impressed by politicians, but they're still interested in public issues.

For some commentators, on the other hand, there can be too much critical scrutiny of elites, even in a democracy in which criticism and accountability are held up as essential characteristics of the political process. Critics have asked if the media, and access programmes in particular, have become too much the occasion for mediated mob rule; 'too free', indeed, 'for an intelligent democracy.'[3] Following Tony Blair's appearance on *Ask the Leader* during the 2001 general election campaign this letter, from a Professor Brian Harrison of Oxford, appeared in The *Times* of June 1.

> Sir,
>
> I protest at the way the Prime Minister was treated in ITV's programme *Ask Tony Blair*. He was placed on a circular platform surrounded by a huge audience, most of whose questioners seemed not only arrogant but blissfully unaware of how difficult it is to run a country. The Prime Minister was cast simultaneously in the role of criminal in the dock and performing animal in a sort of circus. The ringmaster, Jonathan Dimbleby, persistently interrupted.
>
> I hope that many viewers will have shared my admiration for the fact that in these circumstances Tony Blair so patiently and politely struggled to conduct rational and informed argument on serious and complex issues of public policy.

While some may think that Professor Harrison's anxiety on behalf of Britain's most powerful man is a trifle overdone, there can be no doubt that the tone of the audience participation on this programme was, to say the least, 'full and frank'. On the other hand, it must be precisely the unscripted, unpredictable, unrehearsed nature of these exchanges, and what they tell us as a result (and, if he is listening, tell Tony Blair) about the state of public opinion that gives access programming much of its democratic value. As the editor of *Ask the Prime Minister* puts it:

> Shouldn't there be a place on TV for the Prime Minister of the United Kingdom to stand up in front of an audience which duplicates the population at large, and answer in a democratic form a sequence of questions about fundamental issues facing the country?

South East Essex College
of Arts & Technology
Luker Road, Southend-on-Sea Essex SS1 1ND
Tel:(01702) 220400 Fax:(01702) 432320 Minicom: (01702) 220642

63

Richard Tait, speaking as editor-in-chief of ITN, argues that:

> The Carlton monarchy debate was criticised by some for its raucous atmosphere, but it persuaded eight million people to watch arguments about the role of the monarchy and the British constitution when a conventional current affairs programme dealing with that subject would have risked ratings oblivion in peak time.[4]

One measure of the authenticity of such an encounter must be the extent to which it makes room not just for the opinions, but for the language and the debating style of ordinary people. Tony Blair appears to understand this, and is the first Prime Minister to submit to this form of popular interrogation. In doing so, he has probably ensured that he will not be the last.

The *Ask the...* format was subsequently adopted in programmes involving all the main party leaders produced during the 2001 general election. These were widely welcomed, in the absence of televised leaders' debates, as making an important contribution to the election process. *Question Time*, as we have noted, also hosted debates involving all the main party leaders during the 2001 campaign (special programmes gave the leaders of the nationalist parties in Scotland and Wales the same opportunity). BBC network radio broadcast *Election Call* (transmitted simultaneously on BBC1) and *Nicky Campbell*, whose listeners phoned in with questions to the various leaders as they took their turn live on air. Scotland and other localities had similar programmes for their local candidates. These programmes, often backed up with online question-and-answer sessions, provided significant moments of public access to the political leaders during the 2001 campaign, if only because there were so few such moments elsewhere in the campaign. To an even greater degree than in the carefully-choreographed election of 1997 these programmes provided venues in which candidates met 'real people', as the unsuccessful Tory leader William Hague took to calling the British public from his campaign soap-box. These were the only times, with a few exceptions, when the spin doctors and the news managers had to be left at the door and the politicians were obliged to answer unpredictable questions.

## Access and the mobilisation of citizens

To a greater extent than is the case for any other form of political journalism the information provided though access programmes has a stated democratic purpose – that of mobilising an audience to act on, or at least think about, the issues under discussion, and thus to participate, at whatever level, in the political life of the country. For the editor of *Question Time*, 'what we are trying to do is widen the appeal of the political process', an aim which, at a time of perceived decline in democratic participation, increases in importance.

Mobilisation, in this sense, is premised on the programme-makers being able to generate public identification and engagement with politics. From such engagement, it is hoped, stems knowledge, opinion, and possibly motivation to act politically. If they are to have any hope of mobilising citizens to participate in democratic processes, therefore, access programme-makers must first engage audiences in their programmes, a task which becomes steadily more difficult as the media marketplace expands and fragments. In a multi-channel environment of unprecedented consumer choice no-one is compelled to consume political broadcasting. Some may require little persuasion to follow the twists and turns of debate as it proceeds through the news cycle, day by day and hour by hour. Others need some incentive to opt for *Question Time* or the *Jonathan Dimbleby* show over *The Bill* or Sunday football. This harsh competitive reality, no different for political broadcasters than their non-political colleagues, has been interpreted by producers as justifying the introduction of a measure of theatre, spectacle, and drama into political access programmes, giving audiences a reason to choose them over the many others on offer at any given time. Viewers, it is believed, want to feel that they are participating in an event as opposed to undertaking a civic chore. A researcher on the *Jonathan Dimbleby* show stresses that 'we've got to make our programme seem like it actually is participating in the life of the nation, and isn't some sort of ghetto'.

The aims of the show, as Dimbleby himself defines them, are not only 'to illuminate' the public and 'to test' politicians, but 'to *entertain*' his audience. 'If it doesn't entertain, people won't watch', he points out.

Achieving this level of watch- or listenability means that producers must pay attention to the aesthetic quality as well as the democratic functionality of the access form. A skilled presenter is essential, to negotiate the interaction between citizen and politician in the impartial manner required by British public service broadcasting. He or she must be able to stand up for the former – to be people's advocate as well as objective umpire – when the politician seeks to evade a question or comment. At the same time, a presenter must police the participants in phone-in shows (or the expert panelists on debate shows), so that they are able to make their point coherently, and without breaching the applicable rules of etiquette or taste (being able to handle a racist or sexist caller on a phone-in show, for example).

On *Any Questions?* and *Question Time* the selection of questions, and the order in which these are to be asked, is perceived by producers as crucial to maximising the programmes' entertainment value. In both programmes the participating audiences submit the questions from which the final selection is made. The producers' final selection is based on the balance of topics which appear on the participants' pre-show forms, moderated by the producers' judgment of news value. But, notes David Dimbleby of *Question Time*:

> The audience are not free to decide the questions or the order of the questions, or who I pick to talk about them. Our daily bread is earned not by providing an opportunity for our studio audience to do what they want; it's about providing them with the opportunity to do what they want in a programme which is at the same time attractive to two and a half million people.

Where expert contributors are part of the programme format, their selection is also an important factor in generating entertainment value. Panelists on *Any Questions?* and *Question Time* are often senior government ministers, for example, whose contributions and replies will have political resonance beyond the confines of the programme (and who will often be harried into making newsworthy statements by a mischievous presenter). This contributes to the programme's interrogatory function, of course, but also makes it more of a spectacle.

Not all panelists are senior members of the political class, of course, but they must at least be influential figures in the eyes of the producer. They must also be good performers with strong, even idiosyncratic views, and be able to articulate these effectively. Such production considerations may conflict, as the earlier discussion of *Any Questions?* noted, with the aspiration to have a well-rounded panel (gender-balanced, in that case), but producers tend to view this as a necessary compromise. 'It's a balance between entertainment and authority, isn't it?' suggests the producer of *Any Questions?*

One outcome of the desire to engage audiences has been the expansion of expert contributors and panelists beyond the traditional ranks of professional politics, political journalism, senior public servants and so on. In 1999 the Question Time panel was expanded from the established four-person format dominated by political experts (three party members, usually MPs or ministers, and one non-politician) to five, to make room for a non-professional – someone who, though a celebrity in his or her chosen field, such as entertainment or business, is perceived by the public to be independent of the political class and thus 'closer' to the people. Comedians Eddie Izzard and Jo Brand, and musicians Boy George and Paul Heaton are among the celebrities who have appeared on *Question Time* in recent years, in the hope that the programme's reach might be extended to audiences not usually associated with broadcast political debate,[5] such as younger age groups. The editor Nick Pisani explains:

> We have two people on the panel who aren't politicians, because they can support each other. Politicians are professional, they know how to answer questions, they have all got rehearsed lines. But if you have two other people, perhaps a journalist and, say, a pop star or an athlete, they give each other moral support and represent this wider constituency. It's about trying to make the programme accessible so people don't just think 'Oh God, more grey politics'. They are actually going to have a good entertaining programme to watch.

Citing the appearance of Boy George on an edition of the programme broadcast in 2000, which also included the Scottish businessman Brian Souter (included because of his high profile bank rolling of the then-topical campaign to retain the legislation known as 'Section 28', which prohibited the promotion of homosexuality by public institutions such as schools), Pisani defended the innovation against the charge that it was symptomatic of the 'dumbing down' of political broadcasting in the UK, insisting that 'we only ever ask them on [non-professional politicians] if they have got something to say. We take them out for lunch or we meet them beforehand and go through the issues, and we find out whether they have got something interesting to say'. Not only did Boy George perform very well on the programme, defending the gay community against the attacks of Souter and others involved in the Section 28 debate, but he was judged to be 'very influential in club culture. He has been a down-and-out heroin addict, a junkie. He's been to the wrong side of drugs and come back up the other side, so he has got something useful to say on that. He's got real experience, and he's an influence on young people'. Not all of *Question Time's* celebrity panelists are as articulate under the pressure of live TV as Boy George proved to be on that occasion, but the policy of engaging wider audiences by the inclusion of political outsiders was maintained for the spring 2003 run of the programme, the most recent as this book went to press.

On the other side of the public-politician dialogue which access broadcasting exists to facilitate, the composition of participating audiences is also important. For *Any Questions?*, says Jonathan Dimbleby: 'A good audience that is really sharply engaged creates an intensity in the atmosphere which means that the performers up there on the panel gain'. The ideal public participant, like the ideal panelist, is someone with a clear view, able to articulate it effectively, and thus capable of moving the debate on without the need for heavy handed intervention by the chair.

On *Question Time*, such individuals are identified and cued up by a succession of warm-up processes. As participants gather in the hospitality room before the recording takes place Dimbleby gives them a pep talk, and explains how he wants them to engage with the panelists. He stresses that this may be their once-in-a-lifetime opportunity to engage with the political elite. Says Dimbleby, 'It's very important to persuade the audience that they are not there to be cannon fodder. You've got to give them confidence to speak their mind and to be fearless in doing it.' When participants are seated in the studio one of the producers tries to put them at ease by setting out the rules of engagement: how to draw attention to themselves when they wish to contribute to debate; how robust their critical comments should be, and what standards of language and tone are expected; how they should signal their approval or disapproval.

Producers on the *Jonathan Dimbleby* show prefer participants who 'can put forward their point in as few words as possible, who are very clear, who are straight talkers and don't waffle on or go off on a tangent. They make their point and that's it.' Phone-in programmes such as the *Nicky Campbell* and *Lesley Riddoch* shows are even more dependent on articulate participants, relying as they do entirely on audio communication. A willingness to express sincere feeling is also valued on the phone-in, when the topic under discussion demands it. Sometimes, says one producer, 'I'm looking for people to be emotional on air. I'm looking for people to be angry, looking for people to cry. I'm looking for passion'. In programmes on emotive issues, such as a terrorist bombing in London, producers may prefer the participant whose populist prescriptions on law and order, or the war on terror, resonate with the tabloid reader; on others, such as the protection of the natural environment, the preference may be for a more cerebral caller, capable of making what one producer calls 'Guardian 2 points'.[6]

Access programmes specifically designed for sections of the audience perceived to have been neglected by the genre, such as young people, have developed specialised production techniques. Aimed at a late-night, post-pub youth audience, Scottish Television's *Trial by Night* positively encouraged rowdiness and irreverence. Having been attracted to the studio with the promise of £10 and a free drink, participants were encouraged to engage robustly with expert guests – including politicians such as Conservative MP Teddy Taylor – on controversial issues such as capital punishment. Charlene Sweeney, who worked on the programme both as presenter and researcher, believes that:

> for young people, *Question Time* is probably quite fuddy duddy. It's presented by older people, there are panels and politicians, and it's quite stuffy. *Trial by Night* was really different from that. It was designed to look like the inside of a club. It was meant to be really informal.

The objective of these producers was to make a programme 'that had a political edge to it, but was entertaining at the same time'. Its participatory style was intentionally 'gladiatorial', with political guests surrounded by an audience arranged in a circle.

*Trial by Night* ran for nine seasons, and is judged by its producers to have been a success, influencing the producers of access television for young people elsewhere in Scotland and the UK. Argues Sweeney:

> It's easy to slag it off and say 'it's just cheap television' – which it is, because it costs so little to get all these people in to a studio, stick a few banners on it and away you go – but I think it did actually do a service in getting current affairs topics out to an audience who may not be vastly interested in the other types of programmes like *Question Time*.[7]

## Feeding back

If the producers' desire to mobilise and motivate audiences begins by engaging them in the programmes, a further stage is to encourage their feedback. This enhances the representativeness of the public participation they exist to provide, and thus their value as indices of public opinion. For David Dimbleby, 'the point of *Question Time* is to allow a much wider audience [than is present in the studio] to share their concerns and involvement and get a feel for the microcosm of the electorate'. The realisation of this goal has been assisted by the introduction of interactive media technologies such as e-mail and internet chat rooms, now used by a growing number of access programmes (and some, like *Channel 4 News*, which are not access programmes in the sense we are defining it here, but nevertheless see value in having their audiences participate at some level in the journalistic process – see chapter six). Every *Question Time* now broadcast includes Dimbleby's promotion of the web site and e-mail addresses, as well as a text messaging phone number, followed by his onscreen encouragement to viewers to use them in feeding back. The producers of *Jonathan Dimbleby* and *Ask the Prime Minister* also invite e-mail feedback, though their editor cautions against utopian visions of what the new interactive technologies can do to enhance the effectiveness of the form. 'Tell me what is more interactive', he says, 'than a studio audience. Tell me what is more democratic, more immediate than one politician confronted by a hundred ordinary people who can ask any question they want'. At best, for this producer, e-mail can supplement the participatory experience provided by a well-made programme, but not replace it.

Radio programmes make extensive use of e-mail, not just as a feedback channel, but as a means of identifying topics for future programmes, and potential phone-in participants for those programmes. E-mail, in the words of one producer, 'has changed the way the programme interacts with people'.[8] There are drawbacks in the use of new technologies, of course. Online access is potentially voluminous, and thus difficult to manage. E-mails are harder to screen and regulate than phone calls or faxes. A web-site specialist on the *Nicky Campbell* show observes that 'the BBC has very strict guidelines about how we produce programmes, and the point of the internet is its anarchy. Anyone can say anything they want on the internet'. Once again, the expansion of access – this time technologically rather than culturally driven – does not proceed without challenges to the established conventions of mediated political debate and rational public discourse.

## Infotainment and the economics of access

Producers' efforts to mobilise and motivate audiences are premised on the assumption that good public participation programmes should stimulate and entertain, as much as fulfil the normative goals of representation and interrogation. In this respect political access broadcasting is a form of infotainment, where the entertainment function is supportive of, and complementary to, democratic objectives. To entertain successfully is, *ipso facto*, to engage the audience, an engagement upon which basis the loftier democratic aims of access broadcasting may more readily be achieved. Some commentators argue that these goals are irreconcilable since, as commercial pressures intensify, the demand for audience-grabbing entertainment will always tend to supersede and negate the functions of illumination and interrogation. Commercialisation nearly always leads to a decline in the quality of access provided, it is argued. There is, however, no logical reason why the provision of information, the exercise of critical scrutiny, and the delivery of entertaining radio and television should be viewed as mutually exclusive goals. John Street has correctly observed that 'the traditional boundaries marking where politics ends and entertainment begins no longer hold' (2001). Della Carpini and Williams are among the growing community of political communication scholars prepared to acknowledge that 'entertainment media often provide factual information, stimulate social and political debate, and critique government' (2001, p. 161). True of the media as a whole, this statement of the obvious is especially true for those media – entertainment or otherwise – which explicitly engage with the political. If one aim of access is to motivate and mobilise, then making entertainment of it becomes an important element in an effective programming strategy. The entertainment value of the monarchy debate arose not least from its irreverent, subversive tone, in which the deference and sycophancy traditionally assumed to be the British monarchy's due was undermined before the eyes of the eight million people who watched the programme.

That is one very good reason why access programming ought to be entertaining, whatever else it is. The other reason is more pragmatic. The future of public participation broadcasting in the UK will be largely dependent on the success of programme-makers' efforts to combine entertainment with political debate in ways which attract significant audiences. The makers of access programmes on all the broadcast media – even the BBC, which is publicly funded and thus free from the need to attract advertising revenue – know that in competitive media markets their airtime is a valuable commodity not to be squandered. As a result, even a national institution like *Question Time* has had to fight to maintain its place on the BBC1 schedule. Relegated for a time to the late-night 11 p.m. slot, the programme was brought forward to a more viewer-friendly 10.30 in 2000, where it has remained. Presenter David Dimbleby concedes that while he 'would rather it was 8.30 in the evening, the decision to pull us back [from 11.00 to 10.30] is certainly bucking the trend', and a welcome reaffirmation of the BBC's commitment to public access broadcasting at peak time (normally defined as between 7.00 and 11.00 in the evening). There is no guarantee that the BBC's schedulers will be able to sustain this position, however, and access programme-makers are in no doubt of the need to continue to produce popular, as well as politically useful shows. The BBC's entire political output has faced similar pressures, prompting internal reflections such as those contained in *Beyond the Soundbite* (Kevill, 2002), and the wholesale revamp of its political journalism that took place in 2003. During the debate about these reforms, ironically, it was the mass appeal of non-political public participation programmes such as *Pop Idol* and *Big Brother* that was cited as one way forward. In this context, where public participation is valued both as a good thing for democracy, and an effective tool in the competition for viewers, the future of political access will depend on BBC producers' continuing embrace of the kinds of popularising devices described above.

For Britain's commercial broadcasters, meanwhile, and for the same reasons, a sizeable quantity of political access programming *is* still provided as a worthwhile end in itself. Successful access programmes have political value to a media organisation, functioning as branding devices and as a marker of a channel's quality. For small commercial stations access programmes can be a crucial element in building reputation and visibility in the market. 'It's central to the brand,' argued the head of news and current affairs for Scot FM at the time of our research, 'because the credibility it delivers, the quality of audience programmes like that deliver, are attractive to advertisers. Speech programming can help to build your audience, and the quality of your audience.'

At another level exchanges between the public and politicians produced by such as *Ask the Prime Minister* on ITV, or *Question Time* on BBC1, often become news in themselves, feeding into the political agenda elsewhere in the journalistic cycle. This brings status and journalistic credibility to a media organisation – qualities which are even more important in a competitive multi-channel environment than they were in the days of 'the comfortable duopoly'.

Moreover, commercial channels have public service obligations in respect of the quantity and quality of political broadcasting they provide. Local radio station Scot FM, for example, was required to devote at least 51 per cent of its airtime to speech programming, as opposed to music. That speech had, of course, to be produced in a form judged likely to provide the broadcaster with the audiences needed to justify their advertising rates.

Against this background, the threat to UK access programming, whether on the BBC or on commercial outlets, is not only that it becomes too 'popular' or even populist, but that it fails to be popular *enough*, and that its production on the present scale will cease to be possible on competitive grounds. The scheduling pressures experienced by the flagship *Question Time* indicate that even the BBC, by law and custom more committed than any other broadcaster to the presence of public participation in peak-time political media, needs to be reminded of its democratic obligations.

The effort to maintain spaces for access programming in British broadcasting, and on TV in particular, is assisted by the fact that such programming, as *Trial by Night's* Charlene Sweeney noted above, can be relatively inexpensive. Expert panelists usually receive a modest fee, and studio participants will receive expenses where appropriate. Production staff and studio facilities must be paid for, and star presenters don't come cheap. Nevertheless, an edition of *Question Time*, *Any Questions?* or *Jonathan Dimbleby* costs significantly less than a comparable quantity of drama, news or current affairs. Radio phone-in shows, which may last for two or three hours, are even better value for the cost-conscious commissioning editor, and in the case of commercial channels like Talk Radio (now Talk Sport), the demographic data generated by thousands of phone-in callers can have monetary value to marketing organisations. Access programming has sometimes been derided as unworthy of a quality public sphere, precisely because of its cheapness. But this very cheapness – or value for money, as some broadcasters might prefer to characterise it – may be what saves it in the years to come from the increasingly ratings-conscious schedulers. With the important qualification that access programmes must be sufficiently well-resourced to be able to perform their democratic functions, and that they can attract the ratings expected of their various slots in the schedule, there is an economic incentive for their production at current levels to continue.

Despite the economic pressures, political access programmes continue to be a prominent feature of the British media today. They routinely subject the political elite, up to the level of the Prime Minister, to critical scrutiny of a qualitatively different kind from that to which the British people have been used. This development would not have been possible without regard to the competitive requirements of an increasingly commercialised media marketplace, but ratings pressures have not reduced the amount of access programming available, thus far at least. On the contrary, public access programming is one form of political journalism in which it can be argued that the functions of information and entertainment, the principles of civic duty and commerce, are not in contradiction.

## Conclusion

This chapter and the previous one have explored three broad democratic aims which the makers of public participation programming aspire to meet: *representation* of the people in the public sphere; *interrogation* of political elites; and *mobilisation* of audiences to engage with the political life of the country. In putting these aspirations into practice programme-makers have been obliged to take into account the changing political culture of the UK, and the evolving economics of the media industries. Over time these have tended to intensify the commercial pressures on all broadcasters, whether publicly or privately funded, with the consequence that whatever programme makers are trying to do for the democratic process, access has also had to work as popular culture; as media spectacle; as infotainment, in a ratings-driven media environment.

Reconciling these pressures with normative aspirations has not always been easy, and since the 1940s, as chapter two showed, critics have disputed that it can be done. The evidence presented here, however, leads us to the conclusion that within their acceptance of entertainment as a necessary programming goal, sincere attempts have been made by both public service and commercial broadcasters to improve the quality of the access they provide, and that they have made significant progress in two directions.

First, the demographic range of those accessed has expanded from the 'middle class, white' profile of the *Any Questions?* audience to the more socially representative composition of *Question Time*, *Jonathan Dimbleby* and *Ask the Prime Minister*. Limits on representation remain, as we have seen, especially in the imbalance between male and female participants in phone-in shows, which can be attributed to long-standing cultural conventions as well as to factors such as patterns of mobile phone use. Various screening techniques have been adopted in the effort to redress these biases, but producers are consistent in arguing that they cannot always be overcome without damaging the quality of the programmes themselves.

Second, participants have been encouraged to become steadily more assertive in their interaction with politicians. As opposed to the relative deference displayed by participants on *Any Questions?*, the contemporary standard is more accurately represented by the *Jonathan Dimbleby* show and *Question Time*, where criticism and displays of citizen anger are not uncommon, extending to the unrestrained irreverence of 1997's monarchy debate. If the latter programme was far from typical (and controversial, even in these less deferential times – no attempt has been made to repeat the experiment on other topics), the fact that it could be conceived and executed in the British public sphere is a sign of how far we have come, as a political culture, from the paternalistic era in which *Any Questions?* was conceived.

## Notes

1   A senior broadcaster working outside the BBC notes of *Question Time* that its introduction 'was a very happy accident...a programme created to soak up some spare days of Robin Day's contract' which 'turned out to be a huge success' . Whether this account of its origins is true or not, the circumstances of its creation do not undermine *Question Time's* key role in the development of access broadcasting in the UK.

2   For a detailed discussion of the 'adversarial moment' in political journalism see McNair, 2000.

3   Goodhart, D., 'Who are the masters now?', *Prospect*, May 1997.

4   Comments made at the Stirling access and broadcasting symposium.

5   The producers of *Any Questions?* are less convinced of this logic, although musician Billy Bragg has appeared on the show. Jonathan Dimbleby concedes that 'they might do well in terms of persuading the audience to switch on', and that Billy Bragg was 'terrific. He had his own views, expressed them clearly, didn't care who he was upsetting and had charm and eloquence as well'.

6   *Guardian 2* is the review section of the liberal broadsheet *Guardian* newspaper, where issues such as the protection of the environment are regularly addressed in long, research-heavy feature articles.

7   As a key figure in the production of several access programmes, Jonathan Dimbleby questions the value of trying to involve young people in political participation, mediated or otherwise. 'I think they might be wasting their time trying to engage 15–26 year olds', he says. 'I think that once people start to find themselves with responsibilities like mortgages, families, jobs, they start to take an interest. Most young people tend to become middle aged, and I rather think the same about political television. People are very busy, they have better things to do. When they're young they can go clubbing, they can go out, they can go on holidays. Once they find themselves 25, 26, 27 and getting up to 30 they start to take notice'.

8   The advent of the internet has expanded the reach of access programmes beyond that of their broadcast signal. The *Lesley Riddoch* and *Nicky Campbell* shows may be listened to in Europe or the USA, for example, through web sites, and listeners in those countries can respond by e-mail to what they hear. Access, in short, is being globalised. Of course, this expanded technological reach will involve relatively few members of the domestic public.

# 5

# The Effectiveness of Access

We have seen how, under the influence of changing political, cultural and economic environments (notably the post-war decline in social deference, and the increasing competitiveness of broadcast scheduling on both television and radio since the 1980s) access programme-makers have refined their techniques for motivating audiences, improving public representation, and facilitating more rigorous interrogation of political elites. This chapter assesses their success, or lack of it, in meeting these goals. In doing so we utilise data acquired in the course of interviews with programme-makers, and with those politicians and members of the public who participate directly in the various forms of access programming included in the study. We also draw on focus groups conducted with members of the viewing and listening audience for the programmes selected at random (although some of these turned out to have participated in programmes like *Question Time* and *Words with Wark*).[1]

## Engaging audiences

In addition to these, inevitably subjective perspectives two other measures are taken into account here in considering the effectiveness of public participation broadcasting. Neither is presented as proof that mediated access succeeds in the tasks programme-makers set for it, but they do allow some broad, qualitative judgements to be made of their contribution as vehicles for public participation in political debate.

The first of these is the level of public engagement which access programmes inspire, as indicated by two statistical measures: *audience ratings*, which record how many people are watching or listening to programmes; and the levels of audience contribution, and *feedback*, which programmes generate. The size of the audiences tuning in to programmes are a basic indicator of their success accepted by commissioning editors, advertisers and media analysts. Table 1 (overleaf) shows ratings for all the access programmes included in the study, as provided by programme-makers.

Across the eight access programmes we have studied audiences that ranged from 180,000 for the day-time *Wright Stuff* on Channel 5, to eight million for the monarchy debate special on ITV. The one-off *Ask the Prime Minister* attracted 5.25 million viewers, and *Question Time* some three million. On radio, *Any Questions?*

attracts some 1.8 million listeners spread across its two transmissions (the second of which, on a Saturday afternoon, is followed immediately by the audience feedback programme *Any Answers?*, which attracts a further 1.2 million listeners on average). Nicky Campbell's phone-in show records 3.5 million listeners per week.

| Programme | Channel | Audiences (millions)* |
|---|---|---|
| *Any Questions?/Any Answers?* | Radio 4 | 3.0 |
| *Nicky Campbell* | Radio Five Live | 3.5 |
| *Lesley Riddoch* | Radio Scotland | Not available |
| *Question Time* | BBC 1 | 2.85 |
| *Jonathan Dimbleby* | ITV | 1.4 |
| *The Wright Stuff* | Channel 5 | 0.18 |
| *Ask the Prime Minister* | ITV | 5.25 |
| *The Nation Decides* | ITV | 8.0 |

* Some figures, such as those for the monarchy debate (The Nation Decides) and Ask the Prime Minister, indicate audiences received for one-off specials. Others represent average audiences obtained over a season of programmes. In this case of radio phone-ins such as Nicky Campbell the figures follow the industry practice of calculating the numbers of listeners who tune in at least once a week, for at least one half-hour.

In isolation these figures tell us little, but when viewed as percentages of the total available audience for their channels when they were transmitted they can be judged significant. *Ask the Prime Minister*, for example, received one quarter of the available peak-time audience when it was broadcast in December 2000, even although the BBC's popular soap opera, *EastEnders*, was on air during the latter half of the transmission. It is possible that ITV could have obtained more viewers for that slot had it engaged in competitive scheduling and broadcast a soap or a game show, but having opted to run *Ask the Prime Minister* live at 7.00 p.m. the ITV network chief believes that the size of its audience 'surpassed expectations' against 'pretty stiff competition'. That the 1997 monarchy debate attracted eight million viewers on the same channel, at the slightly later time of 8.00 p.m., was also considered a success by senior ITV staff, and an endorsement of their decision to commission the controversial programme.

None of the other access programmes we studied attract audiences of this size, but in the context of their place in the schedule (and the place of their channels in the media marketplace) all enjoyed respectable audiences. Furthermore, audiences for at least some of the programmes have increased over time. Overall, these figures show that British broadcasters *do* routinely engage a significant proportion of the population in mediated political debate, with ten million viewers and listeners tuning in to these programmes in an average week during our research period. Many of these will be the politically interested, relatively easily motivated and regularly taking more than one of the programmes in their weekly consumption of TV and radio (so that the total number of those who watch or listen to access programmes will be less than ten million), but the existence of a sizeable constituency for this kind of political broadcasting is not in doubt.

Audiences for access programmes broadcast during the 2001 general election were low, although consistent with the poor ratings recorded for political broadcasting as a whole, and with the record low turnout on polling day. A *Question Time* debate featuring Conservative leader William Hague attracted only 2.9 million viewers, while *Jonathan Dimbleby's* interrogation of the Liberal Democrat leader Charles Kennedy attracted only 830,000 viewers.

There is scope for debate on what size of audience is consistent with a healthy political culture of democratically engaged individuals. Is the fact that 5.25 million people tuned in to watch Tony Blair being grilled on *Ask the Prime Minister* a genuine broadcasting achievement, as its producers would claim, or evidence of just how disengaged and alienated from politics the population in general is, given that more than three times that number preferred to watch the popular soap opera *EastEnders*? Is there, from a normative perspective, an optimum audience for political broadcasting? Answers to these questions depend on broader assumptions about what it is reasonable to expect people to do with their free time. They cannot be considered independently, either, of the political environment at a given moment. In December 2000, when Blair attracted 5.25 million viewers, there was no political crisis or drama. Had this exercise in public access to the prime minister been conducted in a post-September 11 environment, or as British troops were heading for the Gulf in January 2003, viewing figures may well have been higher. People's interest and engagement in political broadcasting, like their willingness to participate in any form of political activity, can be assumed to be at least partly connected to their perceptions of the state of the political sphere, and their calculation of what it means to them, personally. ITN's former editor-in-chief Richard Tait has speculated that the low ratings recorded by the 2001 election access specials could have been a reflection of the perception that Labour's victory was assured, and that listening to opposition leaders was therefore a waste of time; or, as the advocates of democratic crisis have suggested, that viewers simply did not trust their politicians (or broadcasters) to produce worthwhile and watchable debate.[2]

One thing is certain, however: before *Any Questions?* came on air in 1948 *no-one* participated in mediated political debate. Now, millions have the opportunity, and a sizeable proportion choose to do so on a regular basis. Occasionally, as during the monarchy debate, political access broadcasting has achieved audiences consistent with the top-rated game shows and soap operas. Across the schedules, week to week, audiences for access programmes have been large enough to justify their place, notwithstanding the regulatory requirements referred to in the previous chapter. It is reasonable to infer, moreover, that a substantial audience for political access programming, across an extended period of time, implies a population sufficiently interested in politics to want to participate, even if only as spectators, in mediated political debate. The fact that in a period of channel proliferation these ratings have remained steady, and in some cases increased over time, allows the further inference that audiences are responding positively to the various strategies adopted by the programme-makers in the effort to motivate and engage them.

## Feeding back

A second, quantifiable measure of the extent to which political access progammes can be said to engage their audiences is the level of audience contribution and feedback they generate. Of *Nicky Campbell's* 3.5 million listeners, for example, between 3,000 and 10,000 are sufficiently motivated to call in on any given day, the volume of calls increasing with the newsworthiness and urgency of the subject under discussion. For an edition featuring the Prime Minister 22,000 telephone calls were registered (of which 700 were answered by production staff). In the course of an average *Nicky Campbell* debate around ten per cent of calls are answered, from which a pool of potential participants is then constructed. On the other hand, listeners to the *Lesley Riddoch* show in Scotland – which has a much smaller catchment area – will often hear the presenter pleading for people to phone in and contribute to the on-air debate.

Levels of feedback do provide programme-makers with an important measure of their success in motivating audiences. *The Wright Stuff's* editor notes that:

> You do get a sense of achievement, when you have chosen a subject and an issue, and you know you have received hundreds of e-mails and phone calls, and you have 7,000 people voting on phone lines and you know that you have touched a nerve, and you know that people are going to discuss this and actually that people are going to go forward and make some informed decisions.

## From mediated access to democratic participation

If we accept that ratings and levels of audience feedback are legitimate measures of the producers' success in motivating citizens to engage in mediated political debate, what do they imply for voting rates and other forms of political participation? Does the act of watching or listening to political access programmes reinforce audience members' sense of being democratically engaged? Does it motivate people to participate in elections and other political events and processes?

There is no way of answering these questions reliably without the kind of large-scale quantitative survey which is beyond the scope of this study. We believe, however, that it is reasonable to assert that audience engagement with political debate on TV and radio, should programme makers achieve it, adds to rather than detracts from the cognitive resources available to the citizen, should he or she choose to use them. Jonathan Dimbleby articulates this view when he suggests from his own experience that:

> You may not change attitudes or prejudices but you're feeding, informing. You feed into the pool of public knowledge and if you're lucky you are

helping people form judgements which are important when it comes to making voting decisions.

In relation to his eponymous ITV programme he adds:

> We talk about apathy and alienation from the political process. I think that these kinds of programmes play a part in retarding that process. I like to think that we re-engage people.

While agreeing that the British people, and especially young people, are becoming increasingly cynical about politics, the editor of Dimbleby's show contends that:

> Programmes like ours have helped to retard that process, because I really do believe that we're not watched by political anoraks. The number of viewers is far too high for that. People don't have to watch us. They switch on, and if they like us they continue watching, and they see political arguments and political propositions being advanced and tested.

To repeat a point made in Chapter One – cynicism about politics will not always be retarded by, and indeed may be an entirely rational response to exposure to politicians in the media, and the resulting impatience with their frequently evasive, obfuscatory political discourse. In this sense, successful access broadcasting may just as easily turn people off politics as much as it motivates them to go out and participate in elections. For that reason, too, levels of mediated participation may indicate far greater public interest in politics than voting levels alone might indicate. A producer on the *Nicky Campbell* programme supplied the following anecdote.

> The European elections come along and the turnout's nine per cent or whatever it is. We'll do a phone in the following day about why you [the audience] didn't vote, why didn't you think it was important? And we get record figures for people phoning in. Election turn-outs decline, and shows like ours are on the increase.

The fact that citizens choose not to vote in a given election does not necessarily imply a corresponding lack of interest in the issues, then. On the contrary, as public participation programmes frequently show, citizens may be very clear in their own minds about why they did not vote for, in the above case, their representative in the European parliament, and may use the opportunity provided by broadcast access to articulate the reasons why. That contribution is of value in itself, not least in alerting politicians to the fact that democratic processes are not engaging citizens in quite the way they are supposed to. They represent a body of evidence, a wake-up call to a political class whose legitimacy depends largely on citizens' readiness to express a vote one way or the other.

## The politicians' perspective

This brings us to a third measure of the effectiveness of access programmes: the extent to which politicians take them seriously. One of the normative aspirations of access broadcasting, as we have seen, is to *represent* the public in the public sphere. To the extent that they can do so access programmes are intended to function as symbols of the citizen's place in a democracy, and to facilitate real dialogue, including critical dialogue, between the public and the political elite. Access programming is rightly viewed by those who make it as a means of enabling bottom-up political communication, maintaining democratic accountability and extending political debate beyond the insider circles of professional politicians, journalists, and academics. In doing so it also becomes an important indicator of 'what the people think'.

David Dimbleby believes that *Question Time* 'is quite an effective way of testing public opinion, not least because of its regularity. It happens every week, and I think that builds up a sort of body of opinion, of what the country is thinking.' 'We know it isn't scientific', says the editor of *Nicky Campbell*. 'We know it's not audited research, but it does give you the mood [of public opinion] most days'. If they share these views politicians will be more likely to use the programmes as a source of information, and to pay quite close attention to what access programmes reveal about the state of public opinion on topical issues. Just as they and their advisers employ pollsters and market researchers to periodically gauge public opinion, they will view what people say about politics on *Question Time* and other access programmes as, to some extent, representative of the views of a broader public.

The evidence on this point can only be anecdotal, but it is clear from our research that at least some of the programme-makers believe they are taken seriously by politicians. Jonathan Dimbleby notes that *Any Questions?* and *Any Answers?* have a combined audience after repeats of around three million, and believes on the basis of his own experience that the policy workers of all the major parties 'pay close attention to how people respond' to the points made by panelists, as well as to the questions asked. The *Any Questions?* audience may not be statistically representative of the British population as a whole, as was noted earlier, nor does it enjoy the largest audience, but it is perceived to be representative of a well-educated and influential section of the public whose opinions matter to political parties seeking to command the agenda.

According to the editor of the *Nicky Campbell* phone in show, 'We understand from advisors, not just to the government but also to the opposition parties, that they do use us as a way of gauging public opinion.' At the time of this interview, the Prime Minister had appeared on the programme four times since his election in 1997, suggesting that he at least considered participation in access broadcasts a worthwhile investment of his time.

Having acquired information about public opinion from access programmes, politicians may choose to factor it into their policy- and decision-making processes, or to ignore it and take their chances.[3] A concrete example of the political influence of access was seen during the campaign for London mayor in 2000. A *Question Time* special brought the main Labour, Tory and Liberal Democrat contenders together on a panel with Labour outsider Ken Livingstone, who at that point in the electoral process was still undeclared as a candidate. Such was the drama of the debate which followed between official Labour candidate Frank Dobson and Livingstone, and so vociferous the display of enthusiasm by the studio audience for Livingstone's contributions that, by his own account, he was persuaded by the experience to enter the race. He subsequently won the election, an outcome for which the views expressed by the studio audience that night must have prepared the Labour leadership,[4] even if they did not feel able to acknowledge it publicly. On many other occasions, according to *Question Time's* editor, political guests have been 'surprised' by 'the passion' shown by audiences on certain issues. 'They didn't realise people thought quite like that'.

## Participation and publicity

Another measure of the extent to which political elites take public participation broadcasting seriously is their recognition of its potency as a channel of political communication, and the resulting willingness of a growing number to take part. Contemporary politics is in large part a performance art, and ambitious politicians have to be comfortable with the media, including the medium of public participation broadcasting. Some are 'good at it', judges one editor: 'They enjoy sparring with the public. It portrays them in a good light. It shows that they're willing to face a bit of democracy between elections, if you like'.

To the extent that the critical scrutiny afforded by access programming is perceived by the public to be genuinely rigorous, a willingness to participate in it becomes a public relations asset to the politician who is skilled and confident in its techniques. It is both an opportunity to display one's democratic accountability, and a powerful tool of self-promotion and/or advocacy. Many senior politicians believe that communication through the medium of access programming is a means of speaking directly to a variety of publics. Says David McLetchie, leader of the Scottish Conservative Party, and a regular participant in access programmes such as *Any Questions?* and *Question Time*:

> Performances on TV and radio are far more important than performances in parliament. I am conscious every time I'm on a relatively high profile programme that my colleagues are watching, that other party members are watching, that the wider media is watching, and that it is part of the continuous assessment of me as a politician. If you perform badly over a series of programmes that is going to affect your ranking, where you stand in the political pecking order. At the end of the day, it's your ability to communicate to the wider world that is important. What gets me plus marks is someone coming along and saying 'I saw you on the telly last night, you were really good'.

Willingness to engage the public in access programming does not merely imply an entirely selfless commitment to democratic accountability, then, but also signals a desire to be seen to be performing well in the public sphere. In the promotional culture which surrounds all contemporary political actors these particular forms of media are perceived as a powerful form of publicity, to be exploited as much as possible. Their frequently live, unedited quality, and the fact that they are, notwithstanding the occasional efforts of minders and spin doctors to exert control over the editorial agenda (see Chapter Four), relatively unspun and unpredictable, gives them enhanced rhetorical value in a political culture where spin is a term of abuse. Public participation broadcasting of the type discussed here places politicians before the people with an immediacy, transparency and directness equalled by no other form of political media. To the extent that audiences recognise this (including, as McLetchie notes, the elite audience of professional peers) politicians' participation in access broadcasting brings not just visibility, but respect, even admiration. To participate successfully in an access programme is, for a politician, a potentially more effective form of publicity than is provided by political advertising (which is perceived by audiences as propaganda and discounted accordingly), straight news journalism (which usually lacks the opportunities for politicians to elaborate on policy), or the more in-depth forms of political journalism such as the adversarial interview (where the opponent is likely to be a skilled interrogator, responding in the context of a specific news agenda). The political messages conveyed though access programming are more likely to be seen as 'the real thing', since they emerge in the context of an authentic display of a politician's accountability.

This communicative power can be used to promote the party line, as Tony Blair has done on *Ask the Prime Minister*, or to establish a more individual political persona which may deviate from that line. Producers report that ambitious politicians increasingly lobby them for the opportunity to participate in their programmes, especially in the run-up to general elections. Ex-Labour minister Clare Short regularly used her appearances on *Question Time* and *Any Questions?* as a political platform, making left-field statements which she knew would become news elsewhere in the political media. On an edition of the *Jonathan Dimbleby* show broadcast on 12 January 2003, as tensions over the prospects for war in Iraq mounted, Short used her appearance on the programme to make clear her anti-war position. By this means she displayed (she hoped) her courage, her independence from the party leadership,[5] and her status as a distinctive political voice.[6] As these and many other examples show, public participation broadcasting in the UK has emerged as an important means for communication and debate not just between the citizenry and the political elite, but between different strands of opinion within the political class. In the latter instance the public is invited to act as arbiter, indicating with its response (prolonged applause in the *Question Time* studio, for example, or the sighs of audience disbelief which might accompany a blatant attempt to dissemble by a panel member) what the British public really thinks about an issue, and thus sending a message to the relevant sections of the political elite.

For those politicians who do submit to the ordeal of public participation programming, on the other hand, the rewards can be substantial. Tony Blair's personal rating improved by three per cent in the days following his appearance on a *Question Time* special in late 2000. All the main party leaders appeared on access programmes during the 2001 election campaign, no doubt hoping that they could repeat the trick. As a rule, senior politicians are now much more likely to participate in public access programming than they were ten or even five years ago. Indeed, in the culture of access which has developed in recent years, a politician's refusal to participate would almost certainly be viewed negatively by journalists and voters.

Of course, the very power of these media appearances carries with it risks. As with the adversarial political interview, in which a politician is grilled by a journalist, participation in public access broadcasting can make a politician look good – accessible, knowledgeable, passionate. But a well-directed audience contribution can also expose his or her weaknesses. As noted earlier, the famous *Nationwide* exchange between Margaret Thatcher and a member of the public about the sinking of the Belgrano during the Falklands conflict in the early 1980s is widely agreed to have damaged the then Prime Minister.

This risk of failure gives politicians reason to be afraid of going into media environments – and public participation programmes are a prime example in the UK – where their control over the agenda is reduced or non-existent, and where they are required to engage, live and unedited, with ordinary members of the public. The editor of *The Wright Stuff* considers that politicians 'don't like this sort of show. They are very nervous of appearing in a format like this.' For this source, the rise of political public relations has meant that 'nobody wants to be accountable. Everyone has got much more secretive and guarded, and I think unwilling to take part in these programmes.'

As we have seen, this is not the experience of most programme-makers, who told us that, in their view, many ambitious politicians are eager to participate in access programming. There are some, however (the names of a number of senior Labour ministers were mentioned to us in this context, which guarantees of confidentiality prevent us from revealing), who prefer to avoid it if they can. Some continue to believe that their elevated status removes from them the obligation to be accessible to the public in this form (Labour's Margaret Beckett, for example, refused to participate in the *Question Time* panel which included Boy George). Others fear that they will be made to look foolish, or be set up by malevolent media professionals. One Labour politician who *has* appeared on *Question Time* expresses the mistrust felt by some members of the political class towards this contemporary variation on what Harold Macmillan famously called 'the twentieth century torture chamber'.

> You go on there knowing you are an Aunt Sally, there to be got at. I don't think it enlightens people about the issues. Programmes with audience participation very rarely deal with the real substance of the issues.

As a consequence:

> I can think of a number of programmes which I will just not go on because I'm not interested in acting as an Aunt Sally for the ego of the presenters and the entertainment of the viewers, when a wholly distorted view of what I may or may not be saying will be presented.

For this politician 'audience participation, in the main, does not lead to very serious debate'. What he means, perhaps, is that all too often it leads to exchanges with members of the public in which he feels under pressure. There are many examples in our archive of programmes in which members of the public have made informed, coherent, often eloquent and moving contributions – 'serious' contributions by any reasonable standard – to the debate. On one *Question Time* special, broadcast during the 2001 general election and featuring Tony Blair, the following exchange on the subject of the government's health policy was such an instance. Health policy was one of the issues on which Blair's first Labour administration was vulnerable, since pledges had been made in the 1997 election campaign and not fulfilled. Shortly before his appearance on the programme Blair had been confronted in public (and on camera) by the distraught relative of a cancer patient who, it was alleged, had been poorly treated by the National Health Service.

> *Questioner in the studio audience*: Your manifesto promises for the health service are very much echoes of four years ago. Given this is a clear indication of your failure to achieve the results you wanted, why should we trust you again?

> *Blair*: We made, actually, pretty limited promises four years ago, in respect of waiting lists in particular. But I've got absolutely no doubt at all we've still got a massive amount to do in the National Health Service ...

> *David Dimbleby* (as chairman, interrupting with a reminder of what Blair had said during the 1997 election campaign): You said 48 hours to save the National Health, didn't you?

> *Blair*: I said 24 hours, in fact.

> *Dimbleby*: Well that's quite a big promise.

> *Blair*: But I didn't say within 24 hours I'd transform the whole of the National Health Service. What I said was ... [Blair goes on to defend his record]

This was followed later in the programme by an intervention from a woman whose child urgently required specialist health care.

> *Questioner*: Will you make a commitment tonight that you will put some funding into the bone marrow registries? Our child is desperately needing a bone marrow transplant. She's gonna die without that. Will you make that commitment and help us save her life?

> *Blair*: I can't give you a specific commitment on bone marrow. I can give you a commitment on health service spending. I'm sure ...

> *Questioner* (interrupting angrily): No, it's not good enough, Mr Blair, it's not good enough. We've heard this time and time again ... [goes on to recount negative experience in securing access to bone marrow treatment on the NHS]. It should not be down to individuals like us campaigning to

get donors on registers. It is not good enough. Your government needs to do the campaigning.

The exchange exposed a vulnerable flank in his government's record, and while his questioner is understandably emotional when describing her predicament, she was nevertheless making what most would regard as an important and valid point, with a power and impact derived from personal experience which eclipsed the professional Dimbleby's intervention. The parliamentarian we quoted earlier dismissed the value of audience participation. His views may be an entirely sincere expression of dissatisfaction at the lack of seriousness in access programming. It may also be the case that the degree of critical scrutiny exercised by access programmes might be rather too intense for some of our elected representatives. That, from the perspective of democratic accountability, is strong evidence that the programme-makers are doing something right.

## Public perspectives

We have interpreted the extent to which people watch, listen, participate in and contribute to political access programmes as a measure of their success in motivating significant sections of the British public to engage in political debate. The fact (anecdotally supported though it is) that politicians take the genre seriously, both as a source of information about the state of public opinion, and as a means of gaining publicity for themselves and their views, has been interpreted as evidence of its perceived representativeness on the one hand, and its authenticity as an arena of critical scrutiny on the other.

But what do the public themselves think? Do they agree with the programme-makers (who, of course, have an interest in asserting the quality and success of their work) that access programmes provide opportunities for open dialogue between citizens and their leaders, and for critical scrutiny of the latter by the former? To answer these questions we interviewed, face-to-face or over the telephone, those who participate directly in the programmes. To obtain the opinions of viewers and listeners, a series of focus groups brought members of the public together to watch and listen to extracts from several of the programmes included in the study (see Chapter One for details). The rest of this chapter presents the findings of this audience-centred element of the research, organised under two broad sets of headings. First, we report what our focus groups think of the principle of public participation broadcasting in general, and their assessment of its role in the democracy of which they are a part. Then, we consider their evaluations of the various approaches to public participation broadcasting described earlier in this work, and the extent to which these confirm or contradict the self-assessments and statements of the programme-makers.

## Why access?

It is a striking finding of our audience research that many people feel excluded, if not from the political process itself (to which they are constitutionally connected through their right to vote), then from the political discourse which underpins and supports British democracy. As a result, across the focus groups there was a widespread mistrust of, even hostility to the political class – a view of them as a breed apart, amply in need of the scrutiny access programming can provide. For one focus group respondent:

> I think politicians have their own way of talking, and the general public don't really understand half of what they are talking about because they have got all their own jargon.

Says another:

> I don't think they want you to understand, and I think that's the problem.

For this reason it is 'important that the public gets a voice as well' – all of the public, regardless of class position and social status. Such views were especially pronounced amongst those who perceive themselves to be relatively uneducated.

> It's always the educated people that get the voice. We need more folk like us that are wanting to get in about it and express their opinions and get answers from the politicians.

This, in admirably straightforward terms, is the democratic rationale for public participation broadcasting: the felt need of citizens to 'get in about it' with their governors, an interaction which access TV and radio permit like no other media. Respondents recognise the publicity value of access programming to politicians, and that many of them appear because 'they want to promote themselves'. None the less:

> I suppose it does give the public a chance to air their views as well as the politicians, although sometimes the politicians try and use it as a soap box sort of thing.

> It's really the only time that you see politicians actually interacting on a stage with the general public.

Says another:

> I think it's very valuable. I think people are much more likely to sit down and watch a programme like *Question Time* than they are to pick up and read a newspaper on that particular issue. I think it's much easier. You can just sit back and watch it. It's the same with listening to the radio.

> I think it catches your eye because they're not just telling you information, they are actually having a debate about it. They are bringing in people from the audience. That could be you or I sitting there. I think that is more appealing than just being told the information on the news programme.

For many of our respondents, then, public participation broadcasting facilitates access to the political process for people such as themselves – 'folk like us' – who feel, whether it is true or not, that they lack a voice in the public sphere.

It is very, very valuable, and for the BBC as a public service broadcaster it is extremely important that they keep information for the democracy [sic] in their programming schedule.

One regular *Question Time* viewer, interviewed following his participation in the programme, expressed his support for the format thus:

It's too easy to dismiss and ignore the whole political scene. It [access programming] is something that brings it back to people a little bit, I think, and the audience participation side of it helps. It's much less formal, and the interaction between the panel and the audience packages the political stuff more attractively, I think. ... It's a way in which a lot of us can buy into a process that's otherwise pretty remote. We've got no access to the politicians or the issues at any time other than the general election, and at least there's a chance to gauge the mood of people.

This [programmes like *Question Time*] is better than it was 20–25 years ago. Then people maybe went to big political meetings, but now it's television, and there's a lot more people will have seen that tonight than perhaps five thousand people in the cinema for an old political rally.

One criterion of their effectiveness cited by our focus groups is the extent to which public participation programmes 'change' things. We noted above the anecdotal evidence that politicians pay careful attention to at least some of the programmes, from which follows the *possibility* that policy might be changed as a result of what the debates reveal about public opinion. As to the power of mediated political debate to change opinions among the audience, one of our respondents (a participant on *Question Time*) asserted that:

I've been influenced by what I've heard and the way arguments have been expressed. I've developed a different view, a different angle on a subject that I thought I had firm opinions on, through hearing a different view of it expressed on these programmes.

We have no way of knowing how representative of the audience as a whole this experience is, nor of what 'influence' means in terms of subsequent political action. As Chapter One noted, we make no claims as to what people go on to do with the knowledge and the opinions they acquire from access broadcasting (though this is an important question, which future research in this field may reasonably aspire to answer). Our aim here was to gauge the extent to which people feel that they have *access* to the information (information about policies and political personalities) which enables them to think rationally about politics, and to make the choice between competing positions on the issues of the day.

## Does access work?

How did our respondents evaluate the relative merits of the various approaches to the construction of access adopted by British broadcasters, and in particular the two key directions in which programme makers have tried to develop the form – the expansion of its representativeness to include broader sections of the public;

and the refinement of its participatory techniques to allow more direct access to, and interrogation of, political elites?

First, it is clear that many members of the voting public continue to feel excluded from the more established forms of mediated access, such as *Any Questions?* and *Question Time*. 'It wasn't folk like us', said one when asked for her reaction to extracts from these programmes played for the focus groups. Of those who participate in the programmes, one working class respondent thinks that 'they are a lot of well-spoken, well-educated people on there. I think the majority probably have got strong opinions and are well-educated.' Those who appear on access programmes are perceived to be school heads, teachers, doctors, graduates; those who do not are the old, housewives, single parents, the homeless, and the working classes in general. Many of our focus group respondents see access to, and participation in political debate as a past-time of 'them' rather than 'us' – 'them' being the educated middle classes; 'us' the 'ordinary folk'. One *Question Time* participant told us that:

> I view all this in class terms. The whole set up [*Question Time*], from walking in the door, showed me it's a certain type of person who works in the BBC. Specifically, it was very kind of West End,[7] comes from a bit of money, a different type of person than I am. I work in higher education but I come from a working class background.

Older respondents were particularly attached to this view, which underpinned much of their comments on access programming. Perceptions of class difference and social hierarchy are real, then, and are important in shaping people's assessments of how effective the sphere of mediated access is in representing their interests. Of *Any Questions?*, one respondent considered the audience to be made up of 'people used to dealing with these kinds of issues'. On *Question Time*:

> People who watch *Question Time*, people who participate in *Question Time* are very unlikely to be representative of the whole nation. It's more likely to be your political class and your middle class. You're certainly not going to get very many young people watching it.

Another agreed:

> I don't think many young people would watch it because unfortunately not enough young people are that interested in politics.

These are not entirely inaccurate descriptions of the profiles of those who participate in the flagship political access programmes. As we have seen, the producers of *Any Questions?* make no attempt to deny the 'white, middle class' character of their constituency. *Question Time* has expanded its catchment area substantially, but still attracts (inevitably) a more than averagely well-educated, motivated, civically engaged individual. The impact of *Question Time* on public opinion was limited, for one respondent, because 'only people who are interested in the actual topic tend to watch'.[8] 'This is probably a terrible generalisation', admitted another, 'but if you are not interested in politics you are not going to watch [political access programming] or listen to it. It's probably a minority that are going to watch or listen to it.'

These comments suggest broad awareness of the fact that public participation broadcasting is still the preserve of the already engaged citizen; the individual who is relatively well-endowed with social capital, feels him or herself to be a stakeholder in British society, and is thus motivated – even empowered – to take part in political debate. Interestingly, some of our working class respondents had been involved in an edition of *Words with Wark* produced by BBC Scotland until 1999, and recalled feeling that they had been excluded from the debate in favour of better-educated participants. We have no way of knowing whether this is an accurate account of how the producers handled their audience on this occasion, and in one sense that matters less than the fact that the *perception* of exclusivity is real, and must inhibit the effectiveness of the programme in reaching and engaging the widest possible audience. Some participants perceive *Question Time* as 'very mediated and very edited'. A studio participant noted that she was 'disappointed in the questions. I felt the questions were very manipulated and very directed.' She recalled being asked by the producers to submit questions on specific themes, which duly led off the programme. Furthermore:

> Paddy Ashdown (former leader of the Liberal Democratic Party) was on the show in order to publicise his book, and consequently a question that led directly to Paddy Ashdown's book was asked on the show. I basically feel that most of those questions were chosen by the editorial team rather than the audience.

Mediation of the public-politician interaction does take place, as we have noted, on *Question Time* as on every other access programme, as a production requirement of good programme making. If studio audiences write the questions, it is the producers who select which ones will be asked on air, and when – in order to give the broadcast structure and flow for its three million viewers. Public participants in the studio debate are self-selecting, but must follow the rules of engagement set out by the chairman and the producer. One focus group member recognised that *Question Time* 'has to be structured and it has to get the points across and also be rational and logical, form an argument'. Mediation is a production necessity, therefore, regardless of how unmediated a particular programme can appear to be to the viewer or listener at home.[9]

Perceptions matter none the less, and the view of the participant quoted above, while not echoed by others we spoke to, suggests that the programme-makers still have work to do in convincing the audience of their programmes' authenticity, and in balancing the appearance of spontaneity in debate against the requirements of aesthetically successful TV and radio programmes. This in turn reinforces the case for the producers' efforts to broaden the programme's audience, for example by *Question Time's* device of expanding the size of its expert panel from four to five members, including one outsider; a non-politician who, though recognisable to the audience, is perceived as being 'one of us'. Our focus groups watched the edition of the programme which featured Boy George and the discussion of Section 28, and in the main responded positively, welcoming the involvement of non-politicians with whom the public could more readily 'associate and empathise'.

> Homosexuality is something that I would want to sit and listen about[sic].

> I suppose more people would be interested in political debate if there is somebody that they actually recognise, rather than politicians who perhaps they never vote for.

> I am not interested in politics one bit. However, that is the type of programme I would watch.

In pursuing the popularisation of political debate shows the programme makers are addressing a felt need for expanded access amongst the audience. Where some journalistic and academic critics see experiments like Boy George on *Question Time*, or the monarchy debate, as evidence of the dumbing down of political debate, many of our working class respondents welcomed the broadcasters' efforts to include 'ordinary folk' in public participation broadcasting. Focus group respondents were aware of the argument that such strategies might represent a deterioration in the quality of access programming – 'the argument is that it is dumbing down, having people like him, that it appeals to mass audiences' – but most were clear that they did not accept this interpretation of the trends. Said one respondent, who had also been a studio participant:

> I think you always get good chat. You always get a general impression. It's quick and it's sharp, and even if you don't get all the way through the subject, if you want to do that then you can go and do independent research, you can look in newspapers.

Of the monarchy debate, the most unashamedly populist example of public participation broadcasting included in this research, many of our focus group respondents were positive, contrasting its accessability with the older, more established programmes. Some agreed with those critics who condemned the bear pit ambience of the monarchy debate, articulating the view that 'it wasn't a debate', but 'light entertainment'. For one critic:

> It wasn't really a good debate if you are taking the topic seriously.

Another criticised the fact that chairman Roger Cook 'couldn't control anything', and described the monarchy debate as:

> The Jerry Springer of political shows – the people placed in the audience, picked specifically for their views. They didn't just say hands up and go for people. They went to particular people who had very outspoken, extreme views. They went straight for them.

Many respondents believed that the transmission of the monarchy debate was as much about ratings as about democracy, although they also recognised that political access programmes, like others, must have an audience if they are to survive in a competitive media marketplace. Others among our focus group respondents identified with its lively, deliberately provocative approach.

> You could understand more what they were talking about, you knew what they were talking about. You knew they were talking about the Royal Family and what they were doing to the country. Or what they weren't doing for their country.

> I thought that was brilliant. That's the kind of thing that gets in audiences. It was more relaxed.

> I think it was a very interesting discussion.

> It was a rabble, but it was an entertaining rabble. It was the sort you would want to sit down and watch.

> I think the likes of that really puts the hackles up on the back of your neck, you are dying to hit them.

The participatory style of the programme was also praised, in that 'there was more interaction between the panel and the audience'. One respondent accepted that:

> It was populist, had a mass audience, and it was entertainment, but I am sure people learnt from it.

For one respondent the style of this programme made for a 'better debate' than those produced by more orderly studio debate formats. Moreover, the emotion and passion expressed by many of the participants was perceived to add to, rather than detract from the quality of the monarchy debate, 'because if someone is passionate about something they will say exactly what they feel'. Asked if passion didn't detract from the rationality of the debate, this respondent replied that:

> I don't think you can get too emotional. If you believe in something you're entitled to be emotional.

Another respondent considered the monarchy debate 'better in terms of representation' than, for example, *Question Time*, not only because its participants were drawn from twenty cities around the UK, but because the debate addressed a 'tabloid issue', accessible to a broader audience than might watch the latter.

A similar mix of views was expressed about phone-in programmes. These, in contrast to the studio debate formats, are perceived to involve 'your average Joes on the street'. Focus group respondents recognised a difference between those who participate in a studio debate such as *Any Questions?*, and those who call in to the *Nicky Campbell* or *Lesley Riddoch* shows. The former were perceived to be more motivated, more knowledgeable, and better prepared – pre-meditated in their determination to participate, confident and articulate in the delivery of their opinions. Phone-in participants, on the other hand, were perceived to be relatively impulsive, reactive, and not particularly knowledgeable. There was a recognition that although phone-in shows might be more accessible – 'I think it's a lot easier for people to express their opinion over the phone than it is to go on the telly. The radio isn't listened to as much as the TV is watched and no-one sees you. You could be in your pyjamas' – the quality of the debate they encourage is often lacking. One respondent observed: 'You listen to it to hear people's stupid opinions'. For another, 'the phone-in format doesn't really have much of a debate. It's just people phoning in with their opinions.'

That, however, is one of the key aims of access – to give access and representation to the people's opinions, for better or worse. Improved mechanisms for access to public participation programmes do not necessarily lead to better debates (however one defines 'better'). The debates constructed on phone-in shows, because they are less governed by rules and etiquette than the flagship studio-bound programmes, will be of variable quality, by their nature: at times lively, passionate and informative; at other times boring and pedantic. Just like people, in other words.

## Conclusion

Chapters Three and Four described the broadcasters' efforts to provide improved public access to politicians and political debate. Not all the outcomes of those efforts have been welcomed by everybody, but as we have seen, the majority of those questioned in our focus groups expressed their qualified appreciation. Some, it is true, view mediated access as an illusory form of public participation in politics, vulnerable to manipulation and exploitation both by programme makers and politicians. These critical evaluations serve as a caution to producers to balance their competing pressures – the need to be entertaining and thus popular on the one hand, against the desire to inform and empower citizens on the other. If one conclusion of this work is that British broadcasters have succeeded in getting that balance about right, there are no grounds for complacency. The twenty-first century audience is media literate, and suspicious, often cynical about the motives of both programme-makers and politicians. They recognise, as we have seen, that access programmes can make politicans more accountable. They believe, too, that the broadcasters themselves have to be scrutinised if the access they provide is to be genuine.

## Notes

1  A BBC Scotland access strand taken off air before this research was undertaken.

2  Comments made at the Stirling access and broadcasting symposium.

3  Programmes like the monarchy debate have also been watched with great interest, not least by the monarchy itself, which would have seen there important warning signs of the need to reform its practices.

4  Pisani recalled that at a subsequent edition of the programme, panelist and Labour minister Michael Meacher accused him of packing the Mayoralty special with a pro-Livingstone audience. On the contrary, Pisani assured him, the anti-Dobson feeling came from Labour supporters, not Tories. 'God', Meacher is said to have replied. "I think you're right'. He didn't realise what was going on amongst the public'.

5    Her statements on access programmes were often controversial, as when on *Question Time* she became the first cabinet minister to break ranks with government policy on the Millenium Dome, and again when she criticised then president Clinton over his behaviour in the Monica Lewinsky scandal.

6    Short's comments on the Dome created a minor political crisis for the Labour government, as the Culture Secretary and the Prime Minister were forced into declaring whether or not they agreed with her opinion.

7    An affluent segment of bohemian suburbia close to the BBC Scotland building in Glasgow where this edition of *Question Time* was recorded.

8    Our respondents did not believe that access programming can change people's minds on political issues, since 'If you are sitting down to watch *Question Time* you are going to have awareness of the different angles of a debate anyway'.

9    *Question Time*, as we noted in Chapter Three, is recorded one hour before broadcasting, and edited only in so far as technical flaws are evident in the production. The programme as broadcast is virtually identical, in our experience, to what one sees and hears as it unfolds live in the studio.

# 6
# E-Access and the Democratic Process

The increase in the number of radio and television programmes offering some form of audience debate has been greatly facilitated in recent years by the emergence of broadcaster websites, with ever-increasing numbers of people using these to seek information and to debate issues. Figures from the Office of National Statistics show that in September 2001 9.4 million households in the UK had access to the internet from home. This amounted to 38 per cent of households (and the figure is considerably higher in 2003). Fifty one per cent of adults in the UK had accessed the internet at some time, with men more likely to use it than women (53 per cent of men had used the internet compared to 47 per cent of women). The number of adults using the internet decreases with age: 88 per cent of those aged 16-24 years have used it compared with only 11 per cent of those aged 65 and over (69 per cent for those aged 25-44 years; 59 per cent for 45-54 years, and 38 per cent for those aged 55-64 years).[1]

The growth of these spaces has been hailed as a welcome corrective to the public apathy towards politics described in Chapter One. The UK government has actively encouraged the development of the internet, seeing it not just as a major economic resource but as an additional democratic tool. The net has emerged as an ideal medium by which government can communicate directly with the public, providing more information to people about a wide range of services, and driving forward 'citizen participation in democracy' (UK e-Envoy, 2001), especially among social groups that currently feel excluded from the democratic process, such as young people. The government is currently devising and developing proposals to promote its use as a political and social resource. These include the oft-repeated aim of ensuring that 'everyone in the UK who wants it will have access to the Internet by 2005' (DTI and DCMS, 2001).

This chapter examines how participation in broadcaster websites might help re-engage the public in the political process. As part of the research project we were granted limited access to personnel working on programme-related websites, and we were also able to conduct a web-based questionnaire that surveyed audience attitudes in the UK to political participation via the net. The survey was conducted in December 2000 and January 2001, in co-operation with the British news programme, *Channel Four News*. There were 436 responses.[2] These findings are also presented here.

## The debate: cyber-optimists versus cyber-pessimists

There are currently two broad schools of thought about the impact of the internet on democratic societies (Norris, 2001). Cyber-optimists emphasise its potential to strengthen the institutions of civil society and encourage greater public participation in the democratic process. Cyber-pessimists emphasise the anarchic nature of the internet and its potential to reinforce socio-economic inequalities. Some theorists straddle these two approaches. For example, Manuel Castells (2001) has recently argued that the net has brought a social revolution in western societies because it allows, for the first time, the communication of many to many, in chosen time, on a global scale. At the same time, he also notes that the potential of the net to herald new freedoms is offset by the 'digital divide' that exists between those with access to the web and those either unable to access the net or incapable of using it. The increasing pervasiveness of the internet in many areas of economic, political and social life, coupled with what may or may not turn out to be a persistent digital divide, demands social scientific analysis of the importance of new technologies for citizenship, democratic governance and identity in the twenty-first century (Giddens, 2002). This is especially true for the study of political communication, where doubt remains as to the likely long-term impact of the internet on participation in the democratic process (Bennett, 2000).

## Cyber-optimists

As chapter one described, the media have frequently been implicated in the growth of public apathy about politics in many advanced democratic countries. This has led some to argue that new ways must be found to curb this 'crisis' of democratic participation. Stephen Coleman, for example, warns that 'new relationships between citizens and institutions of governance must emerge if a crisis of democratic legitimacy and accountability is to be averted' (quoted in Coleman and Gøtze, 2001, p.8). A key forum where such relationships might be forged is the internet, and those websites which encourage public debate of political issues. Prominent political and media pundits have stressed the huge potential of the net for political communication. For Dick Morris, a former strategic adviser to Bill Clinton:

> The net offers a potential for direct democracy so profound that it may well transform not only our system of politics but our very form of government. ... Bypassing national representatives and speaking to one another, the people of the world will use the net increasingly to form a political unit for the future (ibid., p.8).

Academics, too, have stressed the possibilities of the internet and other ICTs (Information and Communication Technologies) in reshaping and reinvigorating democratic institutions and processes. For Coleman and Gøtze they 'offer a potentiality of a new environment for public communication which is interactive, relatively cheap to enter, unconstrained by time or distance, and inclusive' (2001, p.5). Blumler and Coleman identify four benefits that online civic engagement can bring to the political process:

- Transcending Time: On-line debates allow time for reflective debate and a space to develop arguments.

- Transcending Place: Participation can take place regardless of geographical distances.

- Making Connections: Internet chat facilitates contacts between groups and politicians and citizens.

- Democratisation and accessability: Online discussions often involve ordinary people who can push their own agendas. (2001)

Few analysts believe, however, that the net will wholly replace the existing fora for public participation that TV and radio currently provide. On the contrary, the broadcasters are among the leading promoters of online political debate and discussion as supplements to their broadcasts. TV and radio access programmes will often promote further debate and discussion via their on-line sites once the programme has finished. It remains very likely that in the short to medium-term, e-participation of this kind will complement rather than substitute for access broadcasting.

## Cyber-pessimists

Other political actors and academic writers have questioned the value of the net to democratic participation and governance. One major criticism is that the kind of participation message-boards and online debates facilitate have few if any tangible outcomes and that the participation is therefore illusory (Putnam, 2000). Another is that the internet has failed to increase access to policy elites or facilitate public participation in the democratic process (Norris, 2002, p.114). Even advocates of the benefits of new ICTs admit their potential to reinvigorate our democratic lives has not yet been realised. So Blumler and Coleman's contention that 'the internet does have the potential to revitalise our flagging political communications arrangements', is tempered by the realisation that, thus far, 'the record of these efforts discloses a mixture of upsides and downsides' (2001, p13).

With the advent of other ICTs (such as digital TV), it is predicted that 'the incorporation of e-interactivity into the domestic sphere will be the real coming of the age of the net' (Coleman, 2001, p.7). But do key actors (policy-makers, programme-makers and participants) involved in e-participation initiatives and access programming agree with these normative aspirations?

## Political interventions in the e-democracy debate

The UK government has also taken a proactive stance in recent years in exploring ways to exploit ICTs across a range of economic, political and social policies. In undertaking these initiatives, the government has clearly tied its flag to the cyber-optimists' mast. In 1998, the government set up the Office of the e-Envoy to oversee and co-ordinate policy commitments. This is part of the Cabinet Office, and has four broad responsibilities. The first is to promote e-commerce in the UK. The second target is to provide net access 'for all those who want' it by 2005. The third responsibility is to have all public services available electronically, also by the end of 2005. Finally, the e-Envoy also coordinates the government's e-agenda across different departments.

In the summer of 2002, the government published a consultation paper to explore ways to promote e-democracy through the development of e-voting and e-participation. The e-democracy consultation process follows on the back of a number of other major political and constitutional reforms that have taken place in the past five years including reform of the House of Lords and the introduction of regional assemblies in Wales and Northern Ireland as well as the establishment of the parliament in Scotland. As the document puts it:

> The government has a wide agenda to reform the UK's political institutions and to re-engage the public with politics and governance. Hence, an e-democracy policy should be viewed in the context of those political and constitutional reforms, which seek to devolve power, extend citizens' rights and improve transparency and accountability of government and politics …[and] the use of ICT to open new channels for participation in the democratic process between elections. This comprises e-participation of citizens in: the government's policy process; the processes of policy-making and scrutiny by elected representatives; the processes of policy formulation in political parties; and other civil society organisations (2002, pp.6-15).

By promoting such ideals, the government hopes to develop the internet according to the underlying principles of inclusion (a voice for all), openness (electronic provision of information), security and privacy (the internet should be a safe place), responsiveness (listening and responding to people), and deliberation (making the most of people's ideas) (2002, p.17). The government's aims are further defined in the consultation paper thus:

> (1) Facilitating participation means making it easier for citizens to exercise their democratic rights. The objective is to use ICT to make it easier for people to access public information, follow the political process, discuss and form groups, get engaged in policy formation, scrutinise government and vote in elections.

> (2) Broadening participation means bringing a wide range of people into the democratic process. The objective is to make use of ICT to open new channels for democratic participation to encourage involvement by people who feel excluded from the democratic process or are unable to participate.

> (3) Deepening participation means going beyond the single exchange to a more sustained, in-depth interaction. The objective is to make use of ICT

to build strong and active relationships between citizens and all levels of representatives, between citizens and government, citizens and political parties and between groups of citizens (2002, pp.15-17).

While the aims of the consultation paper are laudable, there are a number of potential problems with the government's current approach to e-participation and e-government. First, the consultation paper cites numerous international experiments in e-participation but fails to specify who is using these projects. It does does not appear to draw heavily on empirical research, which is a shortcoming in the cyber-optimists' position more generally.

The second main problem is with the broader programme of e-democracy, which has been heavily criticised by a number of recent reports including one by the influential Public Accounts Committee of the House of Commons. In December 2002, the committee argued that 'people are only likely to use online services if they are easier and more cost-effective to use, more accessible and more convenient'.[3] The report is particularly scathing of the Prime Minister's Office website, which 'scores so badly, because its navigation is inept, because of a lack of attention to detail, because it is poorly maintained. ... and because it allows no provision for members of the public to contact either the prime minister or his office'.

A further problem with the e-democracy consultation paper is that it includes few, if any, details about the role of the UK's leading digital providers in promoting public services on-line. Broadcasters provide the most popular sites in the UK, but government has not thus far harnessed the appeal of these sites to promote the e-democracy debate. This is a serious shortcoming, since broadcasters and programme-makers are thinking carefully about these issues, as the next section discusses.

## The programme-makers and broadcasters

One of the features of public service broadcasting is that it often provides a benchmark or quality threshold for the industry as a whole. Public service broadcasters, in Britain and elsewhere in Europe, unlike some of their commercial rivals, have sought to maintain a large production base in the past twenty years, and although budgets for research and development of new programming formats have come under intense financial pressure, and despite the fact that all broadcasters are under pressure to gain high audience ratings, public service broadcasters still have more opportunities than their commercial rivals to experiment with new programme ideas. Other examples of this quality benchmark are the innovative websites that have been developed in the past few years by public service broadcasters including ZDF and the BBC (Collins, 2000).

The introduction and development of broadcaster websites in recent years has allowed programme-makers to introduce new ways of reaching and involving audiences in television and radio programmes. In some cases, such as the use of webcasting in the UK's *Big Brother*, these innovations have been successful in drawing large audiences to broadcaster websites. The use of these websites to provide education, information and entertainment through online news and current affairs, quizzes, features on television and radio personalities, and political discussions have provided broadcasters with an opportunity to reassert their public service credentials. As one radio editor told us:

> What happens is each programme will have a page, which tells you what the contents of that day's programme are. We'll have a phone-in page and have pictures and details about the subject under debate and, we also have a page for our big guest of the day. You can listen to bits of the programme that you've missed. You can listen to highlights. You'll be able to listen to the latest news, weather, travel updates. We also have a message-board up and running. It is a forum for people to discuss the programme; I'll suggest a topic, and they may or may not stick to that, but what we're doing slightly differently with this programme is that we are actually going to read out messages from the board on-air, which hasn't been done before.

Broadcasters, especially the BBC, are taking the opportunities afforded by the web to examine ways in which they might re-engage those currently disengaged from the political process. For example, Sian Kevill, charged with reviewing the BBC's political output in the aftermath of the low election turnout in 2001, has argued that political programmes are increasingly lacking in appeal to the under 45-year-olds. Kevill's conclusion is that 'the BBC needs to get back in touch with how the people are feeling, how they are living' (2002, p.1).

> The message for the BBC is that, like Westminster, we haven't kept in step with the issues that matter to people, and so we can appear less relevant. People see politics and political coverage as being mainly about white, middle class, middle-aged men being badgered by other white, middle-class, middle-aged men in a secret shared language. It's a symbol of the new political divide: it's no longer 'left and right', it's now 'us' and 'them', and there is a perception that the BBC is part of 'them' along with the politicians and the rest of the establishment.

The BBC is continuing to examine ways of using the net to re-engage people in the political process and to help re-invigorate democracy, with the specific aim of 'breaking the current lexicon of politics by injecting into it the needs and concerns and voice of real people' (Kevill, 2002, p.21). When we discussed with programme-makers the potential of the net to realise these aims and to reinvigorate political debate, we encountered a broad range of views similar to those of the academics outlined above. We found cyber-optimists who would typically stress the innovative ways broadcasters have found to incorporate the web into light entertainment programming, while admitting that thus far they have found it difficult to repeat this success with political programming. We also found cyber-pessimists who argued that programme websites tended to attract those people who had formerly phoned or faxed their contributions to programmes; in other words, those already firmly committed to and engaged with the democratic process. This group tended to downplay the potential for the web to broaden participation and to encourage re-engagement in the political process. The viewpoints of the cyber-optimists and pessimists can be best summed up by the following quotes, both from radio producers on the same programme. For the optimists:

> We broadcast to an audience and a limited number of people will speak on the programme. But we decide who gets on to the programme. The message board allows audience members to speak to one another. They can write for as long as they like and if you want to talk about a programme you can go on-line and do that.

And from the pessimistic perspective:

> First-time callers are the ones we're really looking for. Those are our prize callers. … Some of our regular callers started to fax us. And they'd faxed us because they could no longer get through on the phone. And since the fax has become terribly unfashionable, they now e-mail us regularly. Now they've discovered that doesn't work very often, so the next thing they do is go to our message board, and they'll put whatever point of view they have on there. You know, it's a thing designed for regulars to make particular points of view. They're fans of the show. They're our life-blood if you like, but I've already heard their point of view. As a listener I've heard their point of view.

Another area examined in our research was the process of soliciting public contributions online. Here, we wanted to test claims that on-line debate was less mediated than were radio and television contributions and that it allowed citizens simply to talk to one another without elaborate selection procedures. Our main findings were that on-line debates, like their radio and TV counterparts, were subject to interventions from the production team and an online moderator. As one producer told us:

> There's a group of people called moderators who work at BBC Online and they filter messages for libel, incitement to racial hatred, that kind of thing, and then there's a host on each programme and what the host does is like at a dinner party. Ideally a host will stay out of it as much as possible, if people need a bit of encouragement talking about a topic. If it's veering way off or if say a lobby group, say for fox-hunting or asylum you'll get phone-trees, lots of people will sort of bombard it, if that happens, the host will then come in and say, 'come on, let's get back to the point'. It's supposed to be done in a very gentle way, like a dinner party, so it's interesting because we're no longer the BBC broadcasting to people; this is a space, which we own but it is for people to say what they want.

It is interesting to note here that this producer saw her role as similar to that of a radio or TV presenter, directing the broad thrust of debate by seeking to maintain focus on a selected issue. However, for this producer, the net offered more potential for better quality debate:

> At the moment, we broadcast to an audience, they have a certain amount of participation in the programme, but we still decide whether their phone-call gets to air. On-line, the audience are speaking to one another, they can go on for as long as they like. Apart from offensive language and libel, there's nobody telling you what you can or can't say.

This producer clearly saw the internet as an important means for engaging people in political debate in the future. But to what extent do the people who take part in on-line debates share these opinions? As outlined earlier, one problem with research into political websites and their contribution to the democratic process is the comparative lack of rigorous, empirical studies examining public attitudes to and uses of political websites. While there are many global experiments underway into e-democracy involving citizens' polls, public consultations, etc, relatively little is known about who uses these websites, why they use them, if people feel the sites are an important communicative space and whether there are any tangible outcomes of online polls, debates and consultations. It could be suggested that e-participation experiments disclose less 'a mixture of upsides and downsides' and more an absence of empirical studies examining these important questions.[4] In order to find out more about website users and their attitudes to online political discussion, therefore, we undertook a small piece of empirical research into one website run by *Channel Four News*.

## Voice of the participant: the Channel Four News questionnaire

Channel Four's main news and current affairs programme, *Channel Four News*, has run since the launch of the station in 1982. The programme is produced by Independent Television News (ITN), and is broadcast each weekday evening at 7pm. The programme is anchored by the senior UK newscaster, Jon Snow, and lasts for 55 minutes, except for a shortened version on Fridays (30 minutes). At the weekends, the programme lasts 30 minutes and is normally broadcast between 6.30 p.m. and 7.30 p.m. The programme has gained an international reputation for in-depth, quality news coverage, and attracts an audience of between 1 million and 1.5 million. Audiences for Monday to Thursday are generally upmarket (50 per cent ABC1s),[5] of mixed gender (50 per cent male/female) and are older (44 per cent are over 55 years old) compared to all TV viewing at this time of evening. Viewers for the Friday edition are younger (28 per cent are 16-34 years old; 40 per cent over 55 years old). The Saturday edition of the programme attracts an older audience (54 per cent are 55 years old or over), and the highest proportion of females (54 per cent). It is also the least upmarket edition of the week (49 per cent are ABC1s). The Sunday edition attracts more male viewers (52 per cent) and, like Saturdays, has a slightly older age demographic (52 per cent are aged 55 and over).

The *Channel Four News* website offers viewers to the programme further information about the main news items of the day. The site also provides an archive of transcripts and video footage from previous news stories as well as spaces for viewers to discuss and debate political issues. Finally, the programme offers a daily e-mail service that previews the main news stories to be covered by that evening's programme. The *Channel Four News*/ Stirling Media Research Institute questionnaire ran for three and a half weeks from 20 December 2000 until 13 January 2001. The questionnaire, consisting of eleven questions, was advertised during the programme, primarily in the period 20-24 December, when there were a number of special news reports on information technology and new media. There were 436 responses. The broad aims were to find out audience attitudes to mediated political participation and to access programmes on TV, radio and the net.

One of the main drawbacks with surveys and interviews of online participants is that they often do not constitute a representative sample of the general public or internet users. On-line political surveys tend to attract those most committed to the democratic process. To help prevent this, we ran the survey for nearly one month to gather a sample that adequately represents all visitors to that site. Careful consideration was also given to the design of the survey to encourage a good response rate and therefore improve the reliability of the data.[6]

In terms of basic demographic data, we received responses from people representing a broad range of socio-economic groups, although high-income earners were slightly over-represented. One surprising finding was the heavy under-representation of women in our survey. Seventy eight per cent of respondents were male, despite the fact that they constitute only around 50 per cent of the total *Channel Four News* audience. The age profile of our respondents was young, with 71 per cent aged between 16 and 44 (which broadly collates with the latest figures for internet usage). Respondents came from all parts of the UK, although figures for London and the Home Counties were disproportionately high (South East, 21.3 per cent; London, 16.5 per cent; and Scotland, 12.2 per cent registered the highest regional percentages). Eighty six per cent of respondents classified themselves as British White.

Many of our respondents were active participants in the democratic process. 36.2 per cent regularly (at least once a month) listened to radio studio debates such as *Any Questions?*, with 58 per cent watching TV studio debates (such as, *Question Time*). 78 per cent voted in the 1997 General Election (compared to the national average of 71 per cent), and 70 per cent stated that they had voted in their last local elections (compared to a national average of 35 per cent). Thirty three per cent of our respondents had contacted their local MP or councillor in the past year, and 53 per cent had signed a petition in the past twelve months. Twenty three per cent of respondents had contacted TV and radio political access programmes in the previous year as a potential studio member or phone-in caller: 8 per cent of respondents had contacted studio debating programme; 5.5 per cent radio phone-ins; 4.4 per cent radio studio debates. Of those who had requested to take part in forms of access programming (102 people), 52 per cent had done so between two and five times, and four people more than ten times. We found a high percentage of people who sought repeatedly to participate in political access strands. Unsurprisingly (bearing in mind this was an internet poll), e-mail was the stated preferred method for contacting broadcasters (94 people), although a small percentage of respondents used other methods (phone, letter, fax). The four principal reasons cited for requests to participate in access programmes were: to contribute to debates; to balance debate; a general interest in the subject matter; and to acquire direct experience of the subject under debate. Only twelve of the 102 people were selected to take part in a programme or had their contribution read out on air.

The next set of questions related to political participation in website chat rooms or message boards. We asked 'Have you ever taken part in a website discussion? If you have taken part in website discussions, what motivated you to participate?' We found that 23 per cent of respondents had taken part in one or more chat-room discussions or had posted messages. The main reasons cited by our respondents for taking part in such debates were: a strong interest in the subject matter; to seek more in-depth debate; the attractiveness of anonymised participation; and ease of participation from home. Some participants were merely curious to take part in an on-line debate.

We next asked, 'Do you feel website discussions boards are a useful addition to the political process and why?' Here, 171 people responded 'Yes' and 62 said 'No'. Many argued that discussion boards provided a platform for public opinion to be aired and expressed, while others felt that websites provided a low-cost method of participation. Some respondents were attracted to the way websites provided contact with people in the news. However, others (62) believed that websites and discussion boards had no discernible impact on the political process and some argued that message boards only provided an outlet for opinionated people.

Support for this last point also comes in the shape of evidence from Scottish-based studies into the development of e-participation in a newly devolved Scotland. In recent research undertaken by the Stirling Media Research Institute (SMRI, 2001), analysis of the web traffic data to the Scottish Parliament indicated that the Scottish policy community were among the most frequent users of the Parliament's website. The website is also used by those with a work-related interest in Parliament. For the policy and lobbying communities the web allows easy access to political news and information, and to politicians' biographies and registered interests. While it might also provide spaces for public input into policy discussions providing, at times, a measure of popular opinion, evidence suggests the precise patterns of electronic information-seeking behaviour for political websites involve groups already deeply attached to the political process. The report concludes that, as of this writing, considerable doubt remains as to the usefulness of the web for communication between politicians and the general public.

## The effectiveness of the net

Despite the limits of this research, our survey results give us useful information about who accesses political websites, and the reasons for their participation. They also help us examine whether, in the short term, the emergence of the internet is likely to help reverse or even retard the current downturn in traditional forms of participation. Evidence from our survey is that political websites and discussion boards tend to facilitate talk between citizens and groups already heavily involved in, and committed to, the political process. This casts doubt on the cyber-optimists' claim that on-line discussions often involve ordinary people, who can push their own agendas or mobilise people currently disengaged from the political process. Far from promoting 'the language of the people', our evidence suggests that the net may reinforce the language of a small group of (male) actors or interest groups, those who already express their views in other forms of mediated and non-mediated participation.[7]

Politicians are also aware that e-participants are not necessarily 'ordinary' members of the public, and that party members and members of single-issue groups are encouraged to take part in access programmes or website discussion boards. The leader of the Scottish Conservative Party, David McLetchie, argues that:

> Many of them will pronounce views on particular issues or, in some instances, have a committed political affiliation, so they are different in that respect from the broad mass of society who, by and large, are relatively indifferent to politics in general. I suspect audiences are people who will actively discuss political issues in their ordinary life because they are interested in current affairs and public affairs. So they are not wholly representative, but they are representative of the active citizens in our community.

Politicians to whom we spoke also tended to downplay the impact of mediated participation on government or party policy development. While not denying that participant intervention (whether through TV, radio or web) could, in specific instances, have some tangible impact on government policy or initiatives, politicians played down their overall impact. As one senior politician argued: 'I think they have limited value in terms of immediate policy development'.

So does our research support the contention that web-based participation attracts those sections of society disconnected from mainstream politics? Evidence gathered for this book tends to question the contribution which the internet can make to re-engaging those people who have already withdrawn from the electoral process. Our survey shows that some in the younger age groups are accessing political websites, but that these are likely to be individuals already committed to the political process. This research is supported by work done by Janet Jones into people accessing the UK *Big Brother* website (Jones, 2002). She collected 19,000 web questionnaires, of which 70 per cent of those responding were 18-34 year-olds. Jones found that those surveyed between the ages of 18-25 are interested in politics but feel disillusioned with party politics. Her conclusion is that broadcasters will need to develop their interactive services to win the hearts and mind of the 'wired generation'.

## Conclusion

There can be no doubt that political websites provide a cultural space for the public discussion of political affairs. But while the promotion of sites is to be welcomed, their addition to existing methods of political communication should not be overstated. The internet could have significant implications for political communication, but the limited empirical evidence assembled thus far, including that from our research, suggests that its impact on the political process is likely to remain marginal in the short to medium-term. Seasoned e-participation watchers commonly viewed the first internet election in the UK as a major disappointment. Stephen Coleman argues that

> Everyone knew that the net was important, but few knew how to use it inventively. Old forms of publicity were replicated within a new medium: parties and candidates set up websites that looked rather like printed brochures or low-budget TV shows or ads for endurance policies. It was the campaign of borrowed content showcased within the glossy new medium (2001, p.7).

While it might be true to say that few knew how to use the net inventively for political campaigning, the potential impact of the net on political communication is clear. Just as it took newspapers a while to learn how to use the interactive and design features of the internet effectively, so political actors are only now beginning to take its potential as a communicative medium seriously. With the government's ambitious aim to achieve universal internet access for those who want it by 2005, it is apparent that the medium will grow in importance in the next few years. But even if universal access is eventually achieved, e-participation should not be treated as a panacea to the current problems of democratic participation. As Peter Dahlgren argues:

> The evidence thus far is that the Net is a tool, a resource for those with political involvement, but that it generally does not recruit large numbers of new citizens to the public sphere. The Net is not likely to counter the 'great withdrawal' from mainstream politics. …The Net clearly offers opportunities for the motivated. The questions today are not so much how the Internet will change political life, but rather, what might motivate more people to see themselves as citizens of a democracy, to engage in the political and – for those with access – make use of the possibilities that the Net still offers. Some of the answers may be found on the Net itself, but most reside in our real circumstances (2001, p.51).[8]

Although political websites should not be expected to resolve the crisis of democratic participation on their own, those concerned for the health of democracy should support their development as one element of an evolving political culture. Part of this development involves the gathering of better empirical survey and interview data on who uses these sites, why, and in what ways they help re-invigorate political debate. As the UK e-Envoy, Andrew Pinder, argues, 'It's not the voting that's important. That's a service like any other service that can be delivered online. What's important is how to get people involved in the political process and developed debates'.[9] Only then will we be able to fully evaluate the real democratic potential of the net.

# Notes

1    Office for National Statistics, *Internet Access: Households and Individuals*, 26 September 2001 (www.statistics.gov.uk).

2    Peter Barron, Deputy Editor, *Channel Four News*, helped write the questionnaire. We would like to thank him, Alex Gatrell and their website support team for their kind assistance.

3    Alexander, A., 'MPs attack £1bn e-government programme', *Guardian*, 13 December 2002.

4    Coleman and Gotze (2001, pp.36-45) outline national case-studies of 'innovative and pioneering' efforts to use on-line technologies to reinvigorate the democratic process. Reading through these case-studies, one is immediately struck by the lack of research into actual public engagement with these new methods of democratic participation. The authors acknowledge that these are experiments with broad normative aims. They also acknowledge that too few people know about them and that governments have thus far failed to integrate them into the policy process.

5    Demographics measure the population in terms of occupational class. For the purposes of this study, the following categories are used:

| | | |
|---|---|---|
| A | Upper middle class | Higher managerial, administrative or professional |
| B | Middle class | Intermediate managerial, administrative or professional |
| C1 | Lower middle class | Supervisory or clerical and junior managerial, administrative or professional |
| C2 | Skilled working class | Skilled manual workers |
| D | Working class | Unskilled manual workers |
| E | Lowest subsistence levels | State pensioners or widows (no other earnings), casual workers |

6    It is important to note that the respondents were self-selecting and, as such, are not representative of internet users in general. Our respondents also appeared to be more than averagely civic-minded. Furthermore, this research only looked at one website – albeit a popular one. We also acknowledge that the principal methodological approach used in this research – a survey of website users from one news programme – is not best equipped to examine some issues relating to the democratic potential of the net. Questions relating to on-line participation and the formation of networks and communities of users, would require a different type of survey or interviews with political activists. Questions relating to on-line civic engagement providing spaces for reflective debate and the source of new ideas and ways of thinking involving people with relevant experience and expertise would require more detailed analytical research.

7    This finding is supported by recent work into the BBC's *Election Call* programme, where the researchers found a 70/30 split in the percentage of calls from male and female members of the audience. Furthermore, there were significant differences in terms of political priorities and interests between male and female callers. The report confirms the basic argument of our research that while access programmes contribute to democratic life, the narrow range of people taking part in them may limit their role in the public sphere.

8    Recent evidence also supports this assertion. The net was used by peace campaigners to organise support for a series of anti-war marches across the world on 15 February 2003 (Perrone, J., 'Working the web: Anti-war coverage', *Guardian,* 20 February 2003).

9    Ranger, S. , 'Online elections by 2007, says e-Envoy', www.Vnunet.com.

# 7
# Conclusion

This study has described the broadcasters' efforts to provide improved public access to politicians and political debate through television, radio and latterly online channels. Not all the outcomes of those efforts have been welcomed by everybody and there are, as with any form of media output, valid criticisms of the form and content of access programming to be made. But if a genuinely democratic political culture is what we wish to see in Britain, then that implies opening up the political media to what we have elsewhere referred to as 'the sound of the crowd' (McNair, 2000), in all its diversity and sometimes raucous vitality. The movement from elite to mass representation in public participation broadcasting, and from obsequious deference to rigorous adversarialism in the interrogatory style of programmes, has contributed substantially to the development of a distinctively British culture of mediated public access to political debate. If in doing so programme-makers have been led to make infotainment of political broadcasting then, thus far at least, they have also preserved its place in a media environment of heightened competiveness.

As we have seen, the public as represented in our focus groups expresses qualified appreciation of these efforts. Public participation programming in Britain consistently generates what a majority of our respondents view as valuable information about policy, personality and style. We have argued, moreover, that access programming frequently subjects the purveyors of all three to a degree of critical scrutiny. Just before this book went to press prime minister Tony Blair was grilled on his Iraqi policy by an angry, combative audience who, among other criticisms, mocked him for being 'governor of Texas' and 'vice-president of the United States' (reflecting perceptions of his allegedly subservient relationship to George W. Bush). The *Newsnight* access special went out just days before the huge anti-war marches of 14 February 2003, and contributed to a mounting sense of crisis around the government's policy on Iraq.

No other liberal democracy subjects its executive leadership to critical scrutiny in this form and with such regularity across both public service and commercial channels. George W. Bush, certainly, was free of such irritations as he prepared for war in the first part of 2003. The Americans have their shock jocks, of course, in which US citizens debate with each other in relatively unrestrained terms, but there is no equivalent of *Question Time* or *Jonathan Dimbleby* on American broadcast channels, far less the monarchy debate (although, to be fair, the Americans went further and actually got rid of the monarchy in 1776). It is hard to imagine US TV organising a live public debate of comparable tone on, say, the powers of the presidency, or the corruption of Congress. No American president has ever subjected himself to the criticism of ordinary voters faced by Tony Blair on *Ask the Prime Minister* or the *Newsnight* Iraq special.[1]

The emergence of mediated access as a feature of British political culture has the added benefit that politicians must now work harder than ever before to project their intended messages to an increasingly non-deferential public, and rarely in conditions of their own choosing. Mediated access is not a substitute for real politics, but an integral part of what real politics has become. For British politicians, engagement with the people through the medium of access broadcasting is an increasingly important factor in the management and conduct of the contemporary political process. Some, as we have seen, deplore that fact, resenting the pressure it places upon them to engage in unrehearsed, unpredictable dialogue with ordinary people. But if one of the consistent criticisms of British democracy has been the self-imposed isolation and aloofness of politicians – particularly those occupying the remote corridors of governmental power – it is difficult not to conclude that British democracy is the healthier for its developing tradition of mediated access.

Is this adequate justification, however, for the public bar-room, gladiatorial tone of the monarchy debate, or for programmes of a similarly irreverent kind yet to be made? Should we be at all concerned about the emergence in Britain of a popular culture of mediated access, within which the language and registers of ordinary people are valued and even prioritised? Is access broadcasting, as some have suggested, becoming too confrontational, too much the occasion for mediated mob rule?

We wish to argue that genuinely representative, rigorously critical public participation in mediated political debate, of the kind which can assist the maintenance of a healthy democracy, necessarily involves the inclusion of a variety of discursive styles and debating conventions. Richard Tait, at the time of our research editor-in-chief of Independent Television News (ITN), identifies a trend towards 'targeted news and current affairs' in British broadcast journalism. He argues that the 'consensus about how you address audiences, the techniques you use, the production methods, is breaking down.'

The evolution of access programming in the UK, though distinct from straight broadcast news, has been consistent with that trend, so that the genre now occupies what we can think of as a *differentiated* public sphere embracing (like other forms of journalism) broadsheet, mid-market and popular (or tabloid) segments. The access genre has emerged as a key sub-sector of the public sphere, servicing many different publics in their engagement with the political elite. This is reflected in the form and content of programmes from the polite register of *Any Questions?* to the more disrespectful tones of the *Nicky Campbell* show and the monarchy debate. Both extremes, and all the variations in style and tone in between, have their place in a mature democracy where the right to vote, and the right to have a public voice about politics, no longer only favours those of particular class, property, educational or other qualifications (gender and ethnicity, for example). The stylistic diversity of contemporary access programming is, from the normative perspective, a democratic asset. To speak of dumbing down or cultural degradation in this context is to go against the grain of a century of democratisation in Britain.

This study has found that programme makers are generally sincere in their efforts to represent the public, interrogate the powerful, and engage the audience. That said, the critical evaluations of some of our respondents serve as a caution to the programme makers to take care in balancing their competing pressures. If there is a crisis of political legitimacy in Britain, as some argue, then it overshadows the work of the political media as well as that of politicians.

All well and good, some will reply. But the development of public access programming in the UK has not prevented a decline in voting rates, and has demonstrably failed to slow down or reverse the crisis of democratic participation. We have rejected from the outset, however, the presumption that mediated participation in politics will necessarily be reflected in voting levels or party membership figures. Media effects are rarely as simple as that. What people do with the information they receive from public participation programming will always be dependent on the content of the information, and the context in which it is received by the citizen. If watching party leaders such as Tony Blair, Charles Kennedy or Iain Duncan Smith on a *Question Time* election special turns people off voting, so be it. The blame for that outcome can hardly be pinned on the broadcasters who have staged the debates and enabled us to see how our politicians perform in these circumstances. Public participation programming may encourage or dissuade people from participating in an election, precisely *because* of what it tells them about politicians. To repeat a point made in the introduction to this work: mediated political participation is not to be viewed as a substitute for 'the real thing' (however one defines 'real' democratic participation), but is complementary to and supportive of it. The fact that, as of this writing, levels of voting in Britain and other democracies were in decline is not inconsistent with a political media which are functioning broadly as they should in a democracy. One might well ask: how much worse would the crisis of democratic participation be if such opportunities for public access to political debate, however limited and imperfect one judges them to be, did not exist? The head of news and current affairs at Channel 4 is not evading his fourth estate responsibility when he argues that:

> If you [the public] are disaffected with the political process, it won't be for lack of information, it will be for lack of belief that the political process has touched your own life. And that is not our responsibility. That lies elsewhere.

Steve Anderson, head of news and current affairs at ITV, agrees that 'We can treat politicians fairly, and we should do, but there is a real breakdown going on in very important areas of the country between the politicians and the public, and we've got to be realistic about how much we can repair that'.[2] On the other hand, our research and that of others suggests that if anyone can repair, or at least assist in repairing, the public-politician relationship, it is the makers of access programmes. As Chapter One noted, Sian Kevill's report on political broadcasting found public support for greater accessibility in political broadcasting (2002), as did Hargreaves and Thomas' ITC/BSC-funded study (2002). The challenge for the broadcasters is to preserve the spaces (including some at peak time) in which those programmes can find substantial audiences, and to do so in ways which meet the changing expectations and tastes of that audience. As the success of *Big Brother* and similar reality TV formats has shown, the British public wishes to participate through the media, in a variety of contexts. Public participation has become popular culture. And if that is the case, and given the imagination and innovativeness of producers, Britain's long-established tradition of public participation in political debate may be about to enter a new phase. On the other hand, commercial pressures intensify all the time, and while regulations exist to preserve news and current affairs, there is no legal requirement on the public service broadcasters to provide access programming. In Richard Tait's view, 'we need some measure of political access programmes. Five years down the line it won't happen unless it's written in to the statutes'. This may be overly pessimistic since, as we have suggested, access programming on both TV and radio can pay its way in ratings terms, as well as performing potentially valuable branding functions. Britain's broadcasters have been in an increasingly competitive situation for at least twenty years, and mediated access survives, indeed thrives, not least because competing successfully means, in the British media environment, being seen to take news and current affairs seriously. It is in the interests of the broadcasters, as much as the British people, that spaces for access programming be maintained. The competitive climate may change, however, as the ramifications of the 2003 Communications Act work on schedulers and commissioning editors. For that reason, the makers of access programmes will need all the support they can get in the years ahead.

## Notes

1  We are not suggesting that the American public sphere is less open to criticism of politicians than that of the UK. On the contrary, the humiliation of President Clinton over the Monica Lewinsky affair, facilitated by live TV coverage of congressional debates and unedited broadcasts of intimate video-taped evidence went far beyond what any British politician has ever had to face, and is unlikely to be repeated here in the foreseeable future. We would assert, however, that the forms of mediated public access to politicians described in this book are, if not unique to Britain, uniquely well-developed here.

2  Comments made at the Stirling access symposium.

# Bibliography

Ast, V., Mustazza, L., *Coming After Oprah: Cultural Fallout in the Age of the TV Talk Show*, Bowling Green, Bowling Green State University Press, 1997.

Barendt, E., 'Judging the Media: impartiality and broadcasting', pp. 108-116 in Seaton, ed., 1998.

Barker, D., 'Rush to action: political talk radio and health care (un)reform', *Political Communication*, vol.15, no.3, 1998, pp. 367-82.

Baudrillard, J., *In the shadow of the silent majorities*, New York: Semiotext, 1983.

Bennett, W. L., 'Introduction: Communication and Civic Engagement in Comparative Perspective', *Political Communication*, 17, 2000, pp. 307-312.

Bennett, W. Lance, Entman, Robert M., eds., *Mediated Politics: communication in the future of democracy*, Cambridge, Cambridge University Press, 2001.

Bentivegna, S., 'Alla ricerca della politica in rete', in Jacobelli, ed., 2001, pp.14-20.

Bimber, B., The Study of Information Technology and Civic Engagement', in *Political Communication*, 17, 2000, pp. 329-333.

Birt, J., *The Harder Path*, London: Little, Brown, 2002.

Blumler, J., Gurevitch, M., *The Crisis of Public Communication*, London, Routledge, 1995.

Blumler, J., Coleman, S., *Realising Democracy Online: a Civic Commons Online*, London, IPPR, 2002.

Bourdieu, P., *On Television and Journalism*, London, Pluto, 1998.

Briggs, A., *The History of Broadcasting in the United Kingdom: Volume One*, Oxford, Oxford University Press, 1962; *Volume Two*, Oxford, Oxford University Press, 1971; *Volume Four*, Oxford, Oxford University Press, 1989.

Burns, T., *The BBC: Public Institution and Private World*, London: Macmillan, 1972.

Carpignano, P., 'Chatter in the age of electronic reproduction', *Sociotext*, number 25/26, 1990, pp. 33-55.

Castells, M., *The Internet Galaxy reflections on the Internet, Business, and Society*. Oxford: Oxford University Press, 2001

Chambers, S., Costain, A., eds.: *Deliberation, Democracy and the Media*, Boulder: Rowman & Littlefield, 2000.

Coleman, S., 'Interactive media and the 1997 UK general election', *Media, Culture and Society*, vol.20, no.4, 1998, pp. 687-94; 'The new media and democratic politics', *New Media and Society*, vol.2, no.1, 1999a, pp. 67-74; *Election Call: A democratic public forum?*, London, Hansard Society, 1999b.

Coleman, S., ed., *Cyber Space Odyssey. The Internet in the UK Election*, London: Hansard Society, 2001.

Coleman, S., Gøtze, J., *Bowling Together: Online Public Engagement in Policy Deliberation*, London: Hansard Society, 2001.

Collins, R., *A future for public service broadcasting?*, Keynote speech given to the Public Service Broadcasting in a Digital Age Conference, Banff, University of Alberta, 8-10 June 2000.

Curran, J. and Seaton J., *Power without Responsibility, 3rd Edition*, London: Routledge, 1988; *Fourth*

*Edition*, London, Routledge, 1991; *Fifth Edition*, London: Routledge, 1997.

Dahlgren, P., 'The public sphere and the net: structure, space and commmunication', in Bennett and Entman, eds., 2001, pp. 33-55.

Day, R., *Grand Inquisitor*, London: Butler and Tanner, 1999.

Della Carpini, M.X., Williams, B.A.: 'Let us infotain you: politics in the new media environment', in Bennett and Entman, eds., 2001, pp. 160-81.

Department of Trade and Industry/Department of Culture, Media and Sport: *A New Future for Communications*, London: HMSO, 2001.

Diplock, S., *None of the Above. Non-voters and 2001 election*, London: Hansard Society, 2001.

Dovey, J., *Freakshow: First Person Media and Factual Television*, London: Pluto Press, 2000.

Franklin, B., *Packaging Politics*, London: Edward Arnold, 1994; *Newszak and News Media*, London: Edward Arnold, 1997.

Freedland, J., *Bring Home the Revolution: How Britain Can Live the American Dream*, London: Fourth Estate, 1998.

Gamson, J., *Freaks Talk Back*, Chicago: Chicago University Press, 1998.

Giddens, A., *Runaway World. How Globalisation is Reshaping our Lives*, 2nd edition, London: Profile, 2002.

Habermas, J., *The Structural Transformation of the Public Sphere*, Cambridge: Polity Press, 1989.

Hargreaves, I., Thomas, J., *New News, Old News*, London, Independent Television Commission/ Broadcasting Standards Commission, 2002.

Harvey, S., 'Access, authorship and the voice: the emergence of community programming at the BBC', in Izod et al, 2000, pp. 159-71.

Herbst, S., 'On electronic public space: talk shows in theoretical perspective', *Political Communication*, vol.12, no.3, 1995, pp. 263-74.

Hibberd, M., 'E-participation and democracy in the UK', paper presented to the Re-visionary Interpretations of the Public Enterprise conference (RIPE), University of Tampere, January 17-19, 2002.

Independent Television Commission: *UK Programme Supply Review, A report by the Independent Television Commission to the Secretary of State for Culture, Media and Sport*, London: ITC, 2002.

Izod, J., Kilborn, R., Hibberd, M., eds.: *From Grierson to the Docu-Soap: Breaking the Boundaries*, Luton: University of Luton Press, 2000.

Jacobelli, J., ed., *Politica and Internet*, Catanzaro: Rubbettino, 2001.

Jones, D., 'Political talk radio: the Limbaugh effect on primary voters', *Political Communication*, vol.15, no.1, 1998, pp. 83-98.

Jones, J., 'Wired, disenfranchised but not necessarily out of touch: youth attitudes towards mediated democracy', paper presented to the MECCSA National Conference, University of Reading, 18-20 December, 2002.

Judt, T., 'Nineteen Eighty-Nine; The End of Which European Era', in *Daedalus* Vol. 123, Autumn 1994, pp. 83-118.

Kevill, S., *Beyond the Soundbite*, London: BBC, 2002.

Kidd, M, Taylor, W., *Television in the Nations and Regions*, London: Independent Television Commission, 2002.

Kuhn, R., Neveu, E., ed., *Political Journalism: new challenges, new practices*, London: Routledge, 2002.

Livingstone, S., Lunt, P., *Talk on Television*, London: Routledge, 1994.

Livingstone, S., 'Television discussion and the public sphere: conflicting discourses of the former Yugoslavia', *Political Communication*, vol.13, no.3, 1996, pp. 259-80.

Lumby, C., *Gotcha: Life in a Tabloid World*, St Leonards: Allen & Unwin, 1999.

Macintosh, A., Malina, A., Whyte, A., 'Designing e-democracy for the information age', Paper presented to the European Colloquium Conference on E-Networks, Piran, Slovenia, September 2001.

McNair, B., *Journalism and Democracy: an evaluation of the political public sphere*, London: Routledge, 2000; 'Journalism and democracy in contemporary Britain', in Kuhn and Neveu, eds., 2002, pp. 189-202.

McNair, B., Hibberd, M., Schlesinger, P., 'Public access broadcasting and democratic participation in the age of mediated politics', *Journalism Studies*, vol. 3, no.3, 2002, pp. 407-22.

Mansell, R., New-Tech Society: Where all citizens should be free to meet', *Times Higher Education Supplement*, 22 February 2002.

Newton, K., 'Politics and the news media: mobilisation or videomalaise', in Jowell, R., ed., *British Social Attitudes*, SCPR, Aldershot, 1997, pp. 151-68.

Norris, P., *Digital Divide: Civic Engagement, Information Poverty, and the Internet Worldwide*, Cambridge: Cambridge University Press, 2001.

Office of the UK e-Envoy, Annual Report, London: HMSO, 2001.

Office of the UK e-Envoy, *In the service of democracy: a consultation paper on a policy for electronic democracy*. London: HMSO, 2002.

Puttnam, R.D., *Bowling Alone: the collapse and revival of American community*, New York: Simon & Schuster, 2000.

Rakow, L.F., 'The public at the table: from public access to public participation', *New Media and Society*, vol.2, no.1, pp. 74-82.

Reith, J., *Into the Wind*, London: Hodder and Stoughton, 1949.

Ross, K., Coleman, S., *The Public, Politics and the Spaces Between: Election Call and Democratic Accountability*, London: Hansard Society, 2001.

Rushkoff, D., *Media Viruses*, New York: Ballantine Books, 1996.

Scannell, P., 'Public Service Broadcasting and Modern Public Life', *Media, Culture and Society*, Vol. 11, 1989, pp. 135-66.

Scannell, P. and Cardiff, D., 'Serving the Nation: Public Service Broadcasting before the War', in Waites et al, eds., 1982, pp. 161-88; *A Social History of British Broadcasting, Volume One: The Pre-War Years*, Oxford: Basil Blackwell, 1991.

Schlesinger, P., Miller, D., Dinan, W., *Open Scotland: journalists, spin doctors and lobbyists*, Edinburgh: Polygon, 2001.

Seaton, J. ed., *Politics and the Media*, Oxford: Blackwell Publishers, 1998.

Shattuc, J., *The Talking Cure: TV talkshows and women*, London: Routledge, 1997.

Smith, A., *British Broadcasting*, Newton Abbot: David and Charles, 1978.

Stirling Media Research Institute, *The Scottish Parliament Communications Audit; Strictly Confidential*, Final Report, Stirling: Stirling Media Research Institute, 2001.

Street, J., *Mass Media, Politics and Democracy*, Houndmills: Palgrave, 2001.

Underwood, D., 'Reporting and the push for market-oriented journalism: media organisations as business', in Bennett and Entman, eds., 2001, pp. 99-116.

Waites, B., Bennett, T., Martin, G., eds., *Popular Culture Past and Present*, London: Croom Helm, 1982.

Williams, R., *Culture and Society, 1780-1950*, 2nd edition, New York: Columbia University Press, 1983.

South East Essex College
of Arts & Technology
Luker Road, Southend-on-Sea Essex SS1 1ND
Tel:(01702) 220400 Fax:(01702) 432320 Minicom: (01702) 220642

115